Spinoza, the Transindividual

# Incitements

**Series editors:** Peg Birmingham, DePaul University and
Dimitris Vardoulakis, Western Sydney University

**Editorial Advisory Board**
Étienne Balibar, Andrew Benjamin, Jay M. Bernstein, Rosi Braidotti, Wendy Brown, Judith Butler, Adriana Cavarero, Howard Caygill, Rebecca Comay, Joan Copjec, Simon Critchley, Costas Douzinas, Peter Fenves, Christopher Fynsk, Moira Gatens, Gregg Lambert, Leonard Lawlor, Genevieve Lloyd, Catherine Malabou, James Martel, Christoph Menke, Warren Montag, Michael Naas, Antonio Negri, Kelly Oliver, Paul Patton, Anson Rabinbach, Gerhard Richter, Martin Saar, Miguel Vatter, Gianni Vattimo, Santiago Zabala

**Available**

*Return Statements: The Return of Religion in Contemporary Philosophy*
Gregg Lambert

*The Refusal of Politics*
Laurent Dubreuil, translated by Cory Browning

*Plastic Sovereignties: Agamben and the Politics of Aesthetics*
Arne De Boever

*From Violence to Speaking Out:
Apocalypse and Expression in Foucault, Derrida and Deleuze*
Leonard Lawlor

*Agonistic Mourning: Political Dissidence and the Women in Black*
Athena Athanasiou

*Interpassivity: The Aesthetics of Delegated Enjoyment*
Robert Pfaller

*Derrida's Secret: Perjury, Testimony, Oath*
Charles Barbour

*Resistance and Psychoanalysis: Impossible Divisions*
Simon Morgan Wortham

*Reclaiming Wonder: After the Sublime*
Genevieve Lloyd

*Arendt, Natality and Biopolitics: Towards Democratic Plurality and Reproductive Justice*
Rosalyn Diprose and Ewa Plonowska Ziarek

*Worldlessness After Heidegger: Phenomenology, Psychoanalysis, Deconstruction*
Roland Végső

*Homo Natura: Nietzsche, Philosophical Anthropology and Biopolitics*
Vanessa Lemm

*Spinoza, the Transindividual*
Étienne Balibar, translated by Mark G. E. Kelly

**Forthcoming**
*The Trial of Hatred: An Essay on the Refusal of Violence*
Marc Crépon, translated by D. J. S Cross and Tyler M. Williams

Visit the series web page at: edinburghuniversitypress.com/series/incite

# Spinoza,
# the Transindividual

*Étienne Balibar*

*Translated by Mark G. E. Kelly*

EDINBURGH
University Press

Edinburgh University Press is one of the leading university presses in the UK. We publish academic books and journals in our selected subject areas across the humanities and social sciences, combining cutting-edge scholarship with high editorial and production values to produce academic works of lasting importance. For more information visit our website: edinburghuniversitypress.com

© Presses universitaires de France/Humensis, *Spinoza politique. Le transindividuel*, 2018
English translation © Mark G. E. Kelly, 2020

Edinburgh University Press Ltd
The Tun – Holyrood Road, 12(2f) Jackson's Entry, Edinburgh EH8 8PJ

Typeset in Bembo
by R. J. Footring Ltd, Derby, UK, and
printed and bound in Great Britain

A CIP record for this book is available from the British Library

ISBN 978 1 4744 5427 8 (hardback)
ISBN 978 1 4744 5430 8 (webready PDF)
ISBN 978 1 4744 5428 5 (paperback)
ISBN 978 1 4744 5429 2 (epub)

The right of Étienne Balibar to be identified as the author of this work has been asserted in accordance with the Copyright, Designs and Patents Act 1988, and the Copyright and Related Rights Regulations 2003 (SI No. 2498).

# Contents

| | |
|---|---|
| Notes on Translation<br>   *Mark G. E. Kelly* | vii |
| The Unity of Transindividuality: An Examination of<br>   Balibar's Philosophical Practice<br>   *Jason Read* | xii |

**Spinoza, the Transindividual**

| | |
|---|---|
| [1] Individuality, Causality, Substance: Reflections on<br>    Spinoza's Ontology | 3 |
| [2] Individuality and Transindividuality in Spinoza | 36 |
| [3] *Potentia multitudinis, quae una veluti mente ducitur* | 92 |
| [4] Philosophies of the Transindividual: Spinoza, Marx,<br>    Freud | 137 |
| Select Bibliography | 192 |
| Index | 194 |

# Notes on Translation

*Mark G. E. Kelly*

What is presented here is principally a translation of the second part of a book by Étienne Balibar that was published in French in 2018, entitled *Spinoza politique: le transindividuel* (Political Spinoza: the transindividual). In addition, this current volume contains as its first chapter an earlier text by Balibar – at his suggestion – to which key reference is made in the later material. Since *Spinoza politique* is itself something of an anthology, each chapter here has a slightly different original provenance.

The first chapter, not found in *Spinoza politique*, was first published as 'Individualité, causalité, substance: Réflexions sur l'ontologie de Spinoza', in *Spinoza: Issues and Directions. The Proceedings of the Chicago Spinoza Conference*, edited by Edwin Curley and Pierre-François Moreau (Leiden: Brill, 1990, pp. 271–85). The conference in question was held in September 1986. This chapter appears first in this book by dint of its superior antiquity and because it is thus referred to in subsequent chapters. The subsequent chapters appear in the same order that they appear in *Spinoza politique*.

The second chapter, 'Individuality and Transindividuality in Spinoza', originates as an essay published by the Vereniging Het Spinozahuis in English as a single bound volume, *Spinoza:*

*From Individuality to Transindividuality*, in 1997, itself a revision of a lecture given by Balibar at that organisation's headquarters in Rijnsburg in May 1993. A version was contemporaneously published in a revised form in French as 'Individualité et transindividualité chez Spinoza' in a collection edited by Pierre François Moreau, *Architectures de la raison: mélanges offerts à Alexandre Matheron* (Paris: ENS, 1996). This revision, with some additions, is the version included in *Spinoza politique*. Given that it differs throughout in innumerable small variations from the original English publication, I have opted to (re)translate the French into English, albeit guided by the original English. We have also opted, with the author's blessing, to restore the first section of the English original, which represents the sole component of the original that had been excised from the subsequent French versions. I have altered this section only in replacing the English translations of Spinoza with Curley's (see 'Issues of Translation' below) and altering Balibar's phrasing occasionally also to accord with Curley's translation, as well as correcting some extremely minor errors of English. The version of the essay presented here differs overall, then, from the original English version in phrasing, and more substantively in the expansion of some remarks on Matheron in the original into a more extended treatment, the introduction of a diagram illustrating a point made in the original version, and the addition of many clarificatory sentences throughout, almost always appended to the ends of paragraphs.

The third chapter, *Potentia multitudinis, quae una veluti mente ducitur*, was originally delivered by Balibar at the sixth annual conference of the Spinoza Society in Zürich in October 2000, and published (in French, by Schulthess) in its proceedings in 2001 (eds Marcel Senn and Manfred Walther).

The fourth and final chapter, 'Philosophies of the Transindividual: Spinoza, Marx, Freud', is a work first published in *Spinoza politique*. An abridged translation by me of this appeared in 2018 in the *Australasian Philosophical Review* (vol. 2, issue 1, pp. 5–25). This version differs in incorporating material excised by Balibar to fit the length requirements of that publication, and I have also taken the opportunity to make many small adjustments to my earlier translation.

All of this work post-dates the material by Balibar published in his 1985 book, *Spinoza et la politique* – which has already been translated into English as *Spinoza and Politics* (London: Verso, 1998) – and which reappears as the first part of *Spinoza politique*. This present volume, then, comprises writing by Balibar about Spinoza after *Spinoza and Politics*. Of course, it does not comprise all such work. In particular, it does not contain the material that constitutes the third and final part of *Spinoza politique*. The prosaic reason for this is that the first two and the fourth chapters of the four comprising this third part of Balibar's French book have already appeared in English translation: 3.1, 'Jus pactum lex', first published in French in 1985, appeared in the 1997 collection *The New Spinoza*, edited by Warren Montag and Ted Stolze (Minneapolis: University of Minnesota Press, 1997); 3.2, 'Note sur la "conscience" dans *l'Ethique*', which had appeared in *Studia Spinozana*, originally published as volume 8 of *Spinoza's Psychology and Social Psychology* (Würzburg: Königshausen und Neumann, 1992), has been translated as 'A note on "consciousness"/"conscience" in the *Ethics*', in Étienne Balibar, *Identity and Difference: John Locke and the Invention of Consciousness* (London: Verso, 2013); and 3.4, 'Les trois dieux de Spinoza', appeared first in English as 'Spinoza's three gods and the modes of communication' in the *European Journal of Philosophy* in 2012 (vol. 20, issue 1, pp. 26–49). Only the third chapter of this third part, 3.3, 'L'institution de la vérité: Hobbes et Spinoza' ('The institution of truth: Hobbes and Spinoza'), first published in 1992, remains to be published in English translation.

Still, this present book may in effect be read as something of a sequel to *Spinoza and Politics*. The reflections published here follow quite logically from that book. There, Balibar begins by examining the politico-historical context of Spinoza's political thought and its development. From the question of politics, Balibar moves towards the question of anthropology, examining the reciprocal constitution of individuals, society and the state. This examination is the background to the present work, the questions of the inherent social and political constitution of the individual, as well reciprocally of the literal constitution of politics and society out of individuals. In a word, we see here an enterprise of political *ontology*, with the ontological firmly at the fore, though, of course, with Balibar, as with Spinoza, ontology is never far removed from its political stakes. Indeed, this present volume can be said to be less political and more properly philosophical, to have shifted the focus away from the historical context of Spinoza's thought, towards contemporary debates in Spinoza scholarship as well as in philosophy more generally.

The beginning, then, finds us somewhat *in media res*. While one does not need to have read the earlier book to understand this one, it will certainly help. And having some familiarity with Spinoza's thought is surely necessary, as this book is concerned in often technical terms with Spinoza scholarship. The least technical chapter in this regard is the concluding one, and readers looking for something more original and less philological should perhaps proceed directly to that chapter first.

## Issues of Translation

In the original, when Balibar provides French translations of Spinoza's Latin from the *Ethics*, these are his own. I have opted when quoting Spinoza in English always to default to the formulations from Edwin M. Curley's *The Collected Works of Spinoza* (Princeton: Princeton University Press, 1985), but have sometimes modified these translations on the rare occasion when Balibar's point requires it. The most significant such instance is Balibar's systematic rendering of Spinoza's use of the Latin word *ratio* in French as *proportion* in the original versions of Chapters 2 and 4 below. This, I take it, is meant to thematise this term in a way it is not typically by translators, in either French or English. There are two obvious options in English to translate Spinoza's *ratio*, viz. the words 'ratio' and 'proportion'. I have opted, with Balibar's sometime blessing, to use 'ratio', as it makes the most sense in English of Balibar's formulations, and also has the virtue, of course, of being the English cognate of Spinoza's own original Latin term. In those instances where Curley does not translate *ratio* as 'ratio', I have therefore amended quotations of his translations accordingly in the relevant chapters.

In the final chapter, when translating terms originally from Freud, I have adopted a somewhat mixed approach, following James Strachey's standard 1922 translation of Freud when it comes to key terms, such as 'ego', since, for all the inadequacy of these translations, they are very familiar to English readers; however, the German *Masse* – rendered by Balibar in French as *masse* – I have, at Balibar's suggestion, rendered in English similarly as 'mass', following the 2004 English translation of Freud's text by J. A. Underwood (*Mass Psychology and Other Writings*, London: Penguin).

# The Unity of Transindividuality: An Examination of Balibar's Philosophical Practice

*Jason Read*

Étienne Balibar is well known enough to Anglo-American audiences interested in philosophy and political theory that an introduction might seem superfluous. However, what I would like to argue here, albeit briefly, is that the texts collected in *Spinoza, the Transindividual* shed enough light on Balibar's particular philosophy and philosophical practice to constitute the basis for something of a reintroduction of Balibar. Balibar is primarily known, at least in Anglo-American circles concerned with philosophy, as initially a student and collaborator of Louis Althusser and subsequently as an incisive commentator on matters concerning citizenship, race, violence and the border; the former is due to *Reading Capital*, arguably Balibar's most famous text for many years, and the latter has emerged in the collections and essays on citizenship, Europe, violence and so on that have been published in translation in the last thirty years. In the first case there is the overwhelming image of influence, the influence of Althusser and also Marx, especially as the two are often combined in the idea of something called Althusserian or structural Marxism, while in the latter the plurality of interventions with respect to the crises of citizenship, borders and war has effaced the unity of any philosophical project or orientation. I would argue that the essays collected in *Spinoza, the Transindividual* challenge both aspects of this reception, in that the collection posits Spinoza as being as much of a central point of reference for Balibar's thought as Marx (which is not to say that Balibar has abandoned Marx's thought or the larger critique of political economy) and, perhaps more importantly, illustrates to what extent Balibar's thought is more than just a series of interventions on the political questions of the moment but constitutes a profound meditation on the ontology of relations and what such an ontology means for thinking and engaging in politics. Which is to say that *Spinoza, the Transindivdual* constitutes the basis for rethinking the unity of Balibar's thought (to borrow a title from Georg Lukács's book on Lenin, another thinker burdened by the weight of influence and the exigency of situations).

Any argument about the unity of these texts confronts an immediate difficulty. Not only are they texts on Spinoza, thus apparently relegating them to the category of interpretation, they are texts that frame Spinoza's thought through a concept coined by, and associated with, the work of Gilbert Simondon. How to make sense of this detour, of this approach to Spinoza through another philosopher's texts? This question opens up the gap between concepts and problems, between the articulation of a term and its underlying conceptual implications. As Simondon defines the term, transindividuality is an attempt to overcome the binary in which the individual, or individuality, is posed against the collective in a kind of zero-sum game, putting in its place an examination of the constitution of individuality and collectivity. It is a term that Simondon coins, but which Balibar argues ultimately can be found at work in Spinoza *avant la lettre*. This is the case despite the fact that, Balibar argues,

Simondon cannot be understood as an interpreter of or even as having been influenced by Spinoza. Simondon tended to dismiss Spinoza as a pantheist, reducing individuals to parts of nature.[1] That Simondon did not recognise his proximity to Spinoza is nothing new: the history of philosophy is riddled with unlikely bedfellows in which proximities are occluded or misrecognised.[2] What is striking is that Balibar's rectification takes a detour of its own. This is first through Alexandre Matheron's *Individu et communauté chez Spinoza*, which in its own way developed transindividuality, albeit without the concept, through an investigation of the relational nature of individual desire and power in the *Ethics*. Matheron does not so much mediate between Simondon and Spinoza, but demonstrate a different genealogy and a conceptual overlap. At the same time that Simondon was rethinking the ontology of the individual, Matheron was pursuing a similar examination on the terrain of politics and ethics. Spinoza, according to Matheron, overcame a longstanding division between egoism and altruism, between the good of the self and that of others. For Spinoza, the pursuit of one's own power or right cannot be separated from the advantages of others, and vice versa. Spinoza's dictum 'Nothing is more useful to man than man' is a statement of an ideal in which the pursuit of individual power, the capacity to act, is not opposed to collective harmony and freedom, but is the necessary condition for it, and vice versa.[3] What Simondon examines at the level of ontology Matheron finds to be already at the level of Spinoza's politics. Despite these differences of approach and problem, Matheron and Simondon share a similar interest in the broader conceptual histories and logics beyond the history of philosophy. In each case, the philosophical arguments against Aristotle or Hobbes, against hylomorphic concepts or the state of war, expand into a broader cultural and political sensibility. The belief in form and matter, in individuals as the entirety of what exists, or in egocentric individual actions as the basis for politics and ethics, expands beyond the debates of philosophers to become a general cultural sensibility. Simondon's and Matheron's books are interventions as much into a broader conceptual logic as they are examinations of specific philosophical positions, which in part accounts for their broad impact.

As Balibar argues, the history of philosophy has often been characterised in terms of division between individualistic conceptions of politics and society that ground social relations in individual choices and actions, most notably in the social contract tradition, and what could be considered holistic conceptions that place society as something existing prior to its individual members. The most famous (or infamous) of this latter tendency are Hegel and Marx, but one could also include Spinoza, especially in the tendency to understand nature as itself one individual.[4] This 'cold war' in philosophy is not only a division between two 'camps', but an asymmetrical one as well. Individualistic perspectives emerged as dominant both epistemologically and normatively, as holism or organicism is seen as not only incorrect but dangerous. In emerging victorious, individualism has not only cast holistic accounts of society to the dustbin of history, it has also made it difficult to interpret those philosophers who refuse or subvert this binary. For Balibar, transindividuality is less a third way, something between individual and holistic conceptions, but an attempt to challenge the very terms of the division, not just rescuing some of the holistic thinkers, most notably Spinoza, from the holistic dustbin, but also making it possible to develop a new way of understanding both the individual and the collective, or, more to the point, the constitution of individual and collective identities. As Balibar writes with respect to the critics of Spinoza's understanding of subjectivity and individuation:

> They ultimately refer to the intrinsic difficulty which readers had (and still have) in understanding a doctrine which virtually escapes (or dismisses) the basic antinomies of metaphysics and ethics which arise from ontological dualism: individualism vs. holism (or organicism), but also the opposite ways of understanding the human community itself, in which either 'intersubjectivity' or 'civil society', 'interiority' or 'exteriority', is given primacy.[5]

As much as Matheron shifts the terrain of the question of individuation from ontology to politics, underscoring that in the current conjuncture there is no discussion of the individual that is not political, he does so by limiting individuation to its political or ethical valences of egoism or altruism. The ethical and political reconciliation of the individual or community is an important part of Spinoza's philosophy, but it comes after, and is in some sense secondary to, the ontological transformation of individuation and relations. Transindividuality is not just an ethical or political value, but ultimately a rethinking of causality, of the way singular things are affected and determined by their relations. There are echoes here of Althusser's original invocation of Spinoza in *Reading Capital* as providing a new model of causality, that went beyond linear (or transitive) causality of an empirical type and expressive causality of Hegel. In that text, causality was a matter of thinking the social structure, the mode of production as immanent cause, as a cause which exists only in and through its effects.[6] Balibar's return to causality is less about an attempt to think the ultimate causality of the mode of production on other structures, but to understand every singular thing as necessarily determined by an intersection of causes and thus the necessary singular nature of every causal relation. To borrow the terms from Althusser's early work, we could say it is a matter of understanding the causality of the conjuncture rather than the structure.[7] Balibar's detour passes from Simondon to Matheron and back to Spinoza, from ontology to politics and back to ontology.

Balibar's detour through Simondon and Matheron is not just a matter of the construction of an intellectual history, not just the history of his engagement, but a theoretical project. Most notably, Balibar refuses the primacy of either the political or the ontological. As much as Balibar understands that concepts of individuality and society ultimately anticipate and prefigure politics, he does not intend to reduce ontology to politics, seeing every understanding of nature and causality to be simply concealing a political agenda. At the same time, however, Balibar does not reduce every politics to an ontology. This places Balibar not only against a more ontological conception of transindividuality, like the sort argued for by Simondon, but also a general 'ontological turn' in contemporary philosophy. A transindividual understanding of social relations and individuation does not by itself prefigure or determine a politics, nor does a politics, such a particular commitment to equality and freedom, necessitate or dictate its own ontology.

To use a term from Balibar's broader work, it is possible to argue that ontology and politics both constitute an 'other scene' to each other. Ontological understandings of individuality and society must pass over into political practices in order to have political effects, while political transformations of society in relation to the individual have ontological effects by being transformed into concepts and relations. Balibar's own work reserves two separate terms for each of these. The first, as we have seen, borrowed from Simondon, is transindividuality, while the second, of Balibar's own coinage, is equaliberty. Like transindividuality, equaliberty is predicated on overcoming a division of the individual and society, of liberty, which is necessarily individual, and equality, which is necessarily collective. As Balibar argues, the proof of this is not to be found in an ontological postulate, but in political history. At the same time as a cold war was raging in philosophy, proclaiming the individual as the *sine qua non* of freedom, the actual history of the cold war was proving a different hypothesis, one that went against its official ideology. As Balibar writes, describing this hypothesis, 'equality and freedom are contradicted in exactly the same conditions, in the same situation, because there is no example of conditions that supress or repress freedom that do not suppress or limit – that is, do not abolish – equality, and vice versa'.[8] Rather than a political critique of ontology, or an ontological grounding of politics, there is a constant shifting from scene to scene as politics and ontology transform and inform each other.

Such an understanding is profoundly Spinozist, in the sense that many readers, especially in the continental tradition, have stressed that Spinoza's thought cannot be reduced to, or categorised as, an ontology or a politics, but must necessarily be thought in and through the way in which an ontology of relations transforms politics, or an understanding of the political force of superstition changes the understanding of reason and the imagination. On this point the continental, French and Italian, reception of Spinoza strongly differs from the Anglo-American reception. While for the most part the Anglo-American reception has focused on the *Ethics* as a metaphysical work, relegating the

*Theological Political Treatise* and the *Political Treatise* to secondary works, Spinoza scholarship in Europe works at the intersection of the political and ontology. Balibar's detour continues this tendency to think politics through ontology and vice versa, although Balibar differs from many of his contemporaries in that he maintains a gap, and detour, of a displacement of the two levels, refusing what could be called a literal identification of the political and ontological. The reason for this detour is derived directly from Spinoza. Understanding transindividuality as a transformation of causality has an epistemological as well as political and ontological dimension. It concerns not just the organisation of relations in political life or their ultimate bases in the qualities of things but also the relations constitutive of knowledge, including the knowledge of relations themselves. For Spinoza, affects and imagination are as transindividual as knowledge and reason. Such an assertion cuts across the individual bias on both sides. First, exposing the intimacy of affective life to its political and social relations, the imitation of affects inscribes a collective dimension to our most intimate experiences. Second, and in an almost inverse manner, Spinoza's insistence on the collective nature of the common notions, that it is humans in the plural rather than the singular individual that thinks, overcomes the bias of the solitary thinker that has been placed at the centre of philosophy since Descartes (as Spinoza puts it, 'Man thinks: Or, to put it differently we know that we think' – *Ethics* Part III, Axiom 2). Both our affects, the intimacy of our desiring life, and knowledge, the autonomy of the intellect, are more collective, more relational and thus less individual than we tend to think. The corollary of this is also true: collectivity, politics, is as much about the organisation of affects and knowledge as they are about power. The affects of fear and isolation, the imaginations of race and nation, are as transindividual as the affects of love and the knowledge of humanity's usefulness to humanity. As Balibar writes, 'Sociability is therefore the unity of a real agreement and an imaginary ambivalence, both of which have real effects'.[9] It is because both reason and imagination, affects and knowledge, are transindividual, or what Balibar refers to as the 'double relation of the transindividual', that a transindividual ontology cannot directly lead to a politics of equaliberty. The transindividual relation poses a problem, that of the relation of affects to knowledge, that can be solved, or resolved, only in specific situations. This combination of affect and idea, of imagination and reason, traverses not only Spinoza's thought on politics but Balibar's as well. As Balibar stresses in his reading of Proposition 37 of Part IV of the *Ethics*, the imaginary constitution of the state stresses identity, an imagined similarity of love and object. It is hard not to see this as prefiguring the 'fictive ethnicity' that underlies national identity and national politics.[10] This imaginary identity is set against the rational understanding of common interest that underlies liberatory politics; in other words, national identity is the imaginary corollary to the rational constitution of the citizen. Balibar's investigations into the intersecting identities of race, class, nation and gender are all attempts to think through the different imaginations and constitutions of sociality in concrete situations, or, in Balibar's term, specific conjunctures.

Such an assertion points to a larger study of Balibar's thought. My point here in this introduction is to make the suggestion that not only is there a unity in Balibar's thought, but that this unity is one in which Spinoza's thought is as important a point of reference as Marx. Far from relegated to the specific subfield of Spinoza studies, the essays collected here are a general introduction to a sustained rethinking of the constitution and conflict of the ambiguous identities of race, nation and citizen. Or, to be more exact, the specific conjunctural analysis of identity and violence of race, citizen and nation are themselves specific individuations of a general problem that could be described as an ontology, politics and epistemology of the transindividual. In stating this, my point is to shed some light on Balibar's specific practice of philosophy as much as its particular theses. Balibar's practice of philosophy is one in which not only is Spinoza read according to the possibilities of contemporary philosophy, as Simondon's transindividual illuminates Spinoza's thought, but the philosophical transformation is turned towards, and informed by, the current conjuncture.

## Notes

1 See Chapter 2 below.
2 For more on Simondon's relation to his transindividual precursors, Spinoza, Hegel and Marx, see Jason Read, *The Politics of Transindividuality* (Chicago: Haymarket Books, 2017).
3 Alexandre Matheron, *Individu et communauté chez Spinoza* (Paris: Les Editions de Minuit, 1969), p. 164.
4 Étienne Balibar, *The Philosophy of Marx*, trans. Chris Turner (New York: Verso, 2017), p. 121.
5 See Chapter 2 below.
6 Louis Althusser, 'The object of *Capital*', trans. Ben Brewster, in Louis Althusser et al., *Reading Capital* (London: Verso, 2015), p. 344.
7 Étienne Balibar, 'Structural causality, overdetermination, and antagonism', in Antonio Callari and David F. Ruccio (eds), *Postmodern Materialism and the Future of Marxist Theory: Essays in the Althusserian Tradition* (Middletown: Wesleyan University Press, 1996).
8 Étienne Balibar, *Equaliberty: Political Essays*, trans. James Ingram (Durham: Duke University Press, 2014), p. 49.
9 Étienne Balibar, *Spinoza and Politics*, trans. Peter Snowdon (New York: Verso, 1998), p. 88.

10 Étiene Balibar, *We, the People of Europe? Reflections on Transnational Citizenship*, trans. James Swenson (Princeton: Princeton University Press, 2004), p. 29.

# Spinoza, the Transindividual

# 1

# Individuality, Causality, Substance: Reflections on Spinoza's Ontology

Spinozist ontology is an enigma, even today, not only in its doctrinal *direction* (its ultimate tendency on questions of theology, wisdom or politics) but also regarding *the object* about which it speaks and which it proposes to seize with its network of propositions, at least if we do not feel ourselves satisfied with the tautology that the object of an ontology of substance is that being called substance. Can we say that the Spinozist substance is an 'object' on the basis that it is clearly not a 'subject' (in the psychological, transcendental or dialectical senses)? This is the question. No matter what word we may use (we could speak in terms of 'reference'), we cannot avoid this kind of question. Spinoza apparently speaks the language of classical ontology, but the extremism of his statements threatens at every moment to break out of categories. Should we, then, consider his philosophy the first major undertaking of a radical critique of this ontology, practically contemporary with its constitution, at the moment when the new 'conception of the world' linked to the emergence of classical science is also being formed? The difficulty arises from the fact that Spinoza, obviously, proposes not only to criticise but also to know something, by constituting a true analytic of substance without discontinuity between the initial identification of its 'essence' and its 'power' at one extreme and the minute description of individual *conatus* and the dynamics of the affects which represent its complete unfolding at the other. Perhaps the best formulation would therefore be this: the object of the Spinozist ontology is individuation, or *the difference between activity and passivity as such*. But this difference, which is only the activity of its own production, is just as much an originary unity. It is immediately 'practical'. However, it must be thought as completely 'natural'.

Could Spinoza (otherwise than by metonymy) define the singularity of this object in words? Could he reattach it to the idea of an ontology, under which notion we have come to think such things? The very invention of this term precedes his work only slightly. However, whether he was familiar with it or not, it would have to have been unacceptable to him, insofar as it implies both the establishment of a distance between the general and the special (or regional) and the dualism of 'specialised' ontologies. In the Scholium of Proposition 40 of Part II of the *Ethics*, Spinoza characterises 'terms called *Transcendental* . . . like Being, Thing, and Something' as confused fantasies born of the human body's inability to distinguish between a multiplicity of images. He categorises them as the same kind of knowledge (or rather misunderstanding) as universal notions (for example, the notion of Man) and contrasts them with 'common notions' which 'are equally in the part and in the whole'.[1] Why, then, have his readers continued to represent substance as a new ultimate kind or as a foundation? We should see an originary disagreement here, but also a difficulty inherent in the system. Perhaps Spinoza in fact had no univocal term to designate 'his' object and to distinguish it from other analytical or speculative objects. This difficulty becomes evident when Spinoza's text is made to confront other discourses that ostensibly figure in the same historical or theoretical space. The conflicts and misunderstandings that appear thus indirectly shed light on the issues.

Spinoza believes he can assert that all philosophy before him (with the possible exceptions of Democritus, Epicurus and Lucretius) has, in one way or another, succumbed to the illusion of teleology, to which he proposes to oppose a causality rigorously exclusive of any final ends. Over the course of the *Ethics*, the idea unfolds that all philosophies, in spite of their differences and their conflicts, are part of a single 'doctrine of final causes'. What supports this bold – and historically very surprising – assertion? It is, above all, the identification of Aristotelian metaphysics with Cartesian metaphysics. In other words, it is the paradoxical idea that one can connect the naturalistic ontology of 'substantial forms', overtly linked to the primacy of the final cause, to the creationist ontology of 'simple natures', ordered by the theological and anthropological dualisms of extended substance and thinking substance, of the intellect and the will, and of the eminent cause and the formal cause, to one and the same problematic.

To discuss this idea in its own right here would be beyond my remit. I propose instead to formulate a hypothesis, which will at first take a negative form. While Aristotle's and Descartes's ontologies are from the outset metaphysics of substance, which means that they maintain a permanent and privileged foundational, imitative relationship with a representation of 'physis' (whence their antithetical conceptions of individuality), Spinozist ontology is not a metaphysics in this sense. In other words, what Aristotelianism and Cartesianism actually have 'in common', beneath the totally divergent representations of nature they construct, is precisely what sets them both apart from Spinozism, for which *natura*, in the final analysis, is not thought as either a hierarchy of sensible forms or as an extension of quantifiable mechanical processes, which is to say not as a field of physical experience in either of the two great historically constituted senses. You may easily appreciate that such a difference (which is actually already noted in the equivocal form of the general title, which presents an ontology as an 'Ethics') is not very simple either to imagine or to explain, especially as this difference does not signify, manifestly, that Spinozist philosophy has nothing to say about *physis* and maintains no relation with it. One cannot ignore the fact that the whole theory of affects, which ultimately leads to the analytics of activity and passivity, is based on a theory of the mode of constitution of the *body* as 'affections' of the *res extensa* and of power peculiar to 'the idea of the body'. And we cannot deal with this with the idea that the theory of the body is an 'imaginary physics', which would resolve nothing since Aristotle's and Descartes's physics also appear to us as imaginary. The nub of the question must lie in the very concept of the relationship between 'causes', 'individuals' and 'substance'. It is here that it can be instructive to discover in Spinoza the admission of an aporia that shows that the problem of physics forms, in a way, an epistemological boundary of the system itself.

## The Confessions of Spinoza's Correspondence and the Aporia of Physics

I take my lead here from two points in Spinoza's correspondence which are situated on either side of his drafting of the *Ethics* and from which it can be supposed – without this supposition being indispensable – that they are separated by a 'refoundation' of his system.

First, let us examine the debate that took place from 1661 to 1665 between Spinoza and Boyle via the intermediary of Oldenburg. The proposals advanced by Spinoza against Boyle's 'childish and ridiculous doctrine of substantial forms' (Letters 11 and 13) and against atomism, concerning the subject of the composition of chemical substances or species, are at first sight Cartesian in inspiration: an insistence on the distinction between primary qualities and secondary qualities, and an assertion that the sensible properties of matter must be explained starting from the configurations and movements of geometrical extension (Letter 6). Yet, if Spinoza never totally adopted Cartesianism in matters of physics, one can think that this discussion would have helped to finally banish it from his thought, preparing the ground for the thesis of Propositions 8–15 of Part I of the *Ethics*, which refers to the imagination as confusing the essence of substance with that of the modes, the numerical distinction of individuals, and the alternatives of the divisibility or indivisibility of the infinity of matter. The back-and-forth of the arguments keeps bumping up against the ambiguity of the notion of the *individual*, which in the philosophical tradition sometimes refers to a 'thing' that is absolutely simple, and irreducible in idea or in practice to any prior elements (whence the paradox of indiscernibles), and sometimes to a 'thing' that is a whole, irreducible to the juxtaposition of its parts and liable to preserve its own existence (hence the dilemma between mechanistic and teleological explanations of the living being).

It is precisely on the issue of the 'parts' of matter and their assemblage in bodies characterised by specific properties that the debate ends (Letters 30–3). Spinoza warns us that he 'does not have this knowledge' that would allow him to 'know absolutely how things really cohere [cohaerent] and how each part of Nature agrees [conveniat] with its "whole'" because such knowledge would have to encompass 'the whole of nature and all its parts'. However, he undertakes an attempt to formulate the principle, and he does so with the precise intention of opposing an adequate idea of the 'whole' of Nature to the imagination of a cosmic *order* ('me Naturae non tribuere pulchritudinem, deformitatem, ordinem, neque confusionem').

The example proposed by Spinoza (the composition of the blood) illustrates the essentially relative character of the notions of 'whole' and 'part' – not in the subjective sense, but in the sense of an objective order of magnitude, which corresponds to the distinction between 'external causes' and 'internal causes' subject to the same 'relations of motion'. We can obviously ask whether this explanation is not tautological, since the magnitude of a given combination (the 'parts' of the blood, the blood itself, the man, the 'medium' of the man, etc.), characterised by interiority (the control of the variations of certain causes: 'quae leges naturae sanguinis certo modo moderantur') and exteriority (the independence of certain other things) is already equivalent to a given individuality. Spinoza does not stop there, and extends this model to the universe, which is to say to an 'absolutely infinite nature'.

Here, the argument divides, in a troubling juxtaposition. On one side, the unity of the parts of the universe can be conceived as a reciprocity of action between these parts: 'omnia enim corpora ab aliis circumcinguuntur, et ab invicem determinantur ad existendum et operandum certa ac determinata ratione'. The condition which allows us to think such a reciprocal action is that 'the same ratio of motion to rest always being preserved in all of them at once [that is, in the whole universe]'.[2] This proposition is almost literally borrowed from Descartes[3] except that conservation is not attributed to the constant action of the omnipotence of God. On the other hand, Spinoza adds that he conceives, *ratione substantiae* (that is to say, because of substance, or in relation to substance) an 'even closer' (*arctiorem*) union between each part and its whole. How should we understand this detail? We can see there the positive counterpart of the omission of the God of the continued creation. But this could be interpreted either as positing a 'unity of substance' that would be *more* (and something other) *than a whole*, or as asserting that *the true* (not relative, so infinite) *totality* can be conceived only as an indivisible substance, which is to say, without 'parts' in the proper sense. Without developing this point, Spinoza concludes that we can, on this basis, understand how the human body and the human soul are each 'part of nature' – specifically the 'corporeal substance' (*substantia corporea*) and the 'infinite power of thinking' respectively, each of these containing the other.

Oldenburg's answer is extremely interesting:

> I do not sufficiently follow how we can eliminate the order and symmetry from nature, as you seem to do, especially since you yourself recognise that all its bodies are surrounded by others, and are mutually determined, in a definite and constant manner [certa et constanti ratione], both to existing and producing an effect with the same ratio of motion to rest always being preserved in all together [eadem semper in omnibus simul motus ad quietem ratione servata]. This seems to be the formal ground itself of a true order [ipsissima veri ordinis ratio fomalis esse videtur].

In other words, Oldenburg, either by naiveté or by malice (he immediately follows this by asking Spinoza to explain again the rules of motion that Descartes thought he could infer from his principle), has raised the strongest possible objection. It implies that, even without reference to divine creation, a principle like the 'conservation of motion and rest in nature' remains a teleological principle, and more generally that any statement about the 'reason of the whole' is the equivalent of a principle of order and symmetry.

We cannot ignore this objection. Not only because Spinoza, in the 'physics' that he will include in his system (or what, in Part II of the *Ethics*, can be read as the sketch of a physics), will continue to refer, if quite hypothetically, to this principle concerning the 'whole of nature conceived as a single individual'.[4] But above all because in the *Ethics*, after having disqualified the concept of order as typical of the teleological imagination, he does not, however, stop using it himself, both in the very formula that his definition of cause develops into (*ordo* and *connexio rerum*) and in his constant reference to 'the order of Nature' – conformity with which is a matter of thinking the chain of singular things and their ideas – not to mention 'geometrical order' and 'the order of the intellect' (or order 'conforming to the intellect').[5] There are therefore at least *two* notions of order, homonymous and yet antithetical, in Spinoza. One can immediately notice the difference in essential effect between these two: one requires a correlative notion of disorder which the other does not at all, any more than a notion of perfection understood as reality calls for imperfection as a correlate. But it is by no means obvious that they do not both imply finality. It is not enough just to say so. Moreover, even if he constantly rehearses the difference between these two notions, Spinoza explains it nowhere, never giving what might be called an adequate definition of order.

Now, Oldenburg's objection touches on a central point in the philosophy of physics. This is the 'break' between ancient physics (which begins with Aristotle) and modern physics (such as we see being constituted with Galileo proving the 'simplicity' of Copernicanism and the laws of motion, and being reflected upon for the first time with the Cartesian definition of 'laws of nature'). This break does not lie in the fact that the former refers to the notion of order or symmetry and the latter does not. It lies rather in the fact that the former applies mechanistic or teleological principles to the explanation of the visible, symmetrical forms directly observable in nature, while the second looks for *symmetry* in mathematical laws themselves (later defined as their invariance for certain groups of transformations). The symmetry of laws does not exclude apparent disorder, which is to say irregular complexity or divergent evolution of phenomena (which depends on 'initial conditions').[6] The Cartesian statement (from which the 'laws of Nature' or 'laws of motion' are deduced) is, despite its vagueness, the prototype of the seemingly teleological principles which assure the coherence and 'simplicity' of physical theory, and which will take the form of laws of conservation or principles of invariance. Without symmetry in this sense, the very possibility of a causal explanation would remain indeterminate. It would therefore not be traducing Oldenburg's retort to read here in retrospect the following alternative: either a science of nature must be guided by principles of order in the search for causes and their (mathematical) determination, or it denies this necessity and claims to avoid it radically by only dealing with 'pure' causality. But then it will never be *a science* in the sense of physical theory (which indeed seems to be the case for the Spinozist theory of the body, this time unlike Descartes's own physics, despite all his errors, not to mention those of Leibniz or Newton).[7]

But conversely, one may nonetheless look in Spinoza for the ingredients of an inquiry directed towards physics (or towards a philosophy of physics). What criteria distinguish *a priori* a scientific concept of order, of 'simplicity' or of symmetry from a theological or metaphysical concept by the same name, hanging on assumptions such as 'nature does nothing for nothing' and the belief in creation or in pre-established harmony? And to what extent does the deduction of laws of nature made by physicists from such principles (experimentally verified though they may be) amount in fact to abstraction, which means that physicists do not know *things* themselves, but only a theoretical 'nature', by hypothesis simplified to coincide with the domain of universal regularities, or situations of experience in which these regularities are approximately realised? What is a 'thing' if it is not the object of an organised experience according to the idea of an order that makes this possible? What we see looming on the horizon of this discussion and its incompleteness is nothing less than the question of the 'principle of reason'.

Let us now turn to the final letters exchanged between 1674 and 1676 between Spinoza, the medico Schuller and the latter's friend Tschirnhaus (also himself a philosopher-scientist, and a correspondent of the Royal Society and Leibniz), who had together undertaken to read the *Ethics*. Despite its apparent disorder, this discussion focuses on three key points, which turn out to be closely linked:

1. What is the nature of the definition of a 'real thing', expressing *the essence* of the thing, or the 'efficient cause' of all its properties (as opposed to the statement of a mere characteristic property)? (Letters 59, 60, 82, 83)
2. Of what does the 'correspondence' between thought and the understanding, and more generally between thought and 'any other' attribute, as mentioned in Proposition 7 of Part II of the *Ethics*, consist? Tschirnhaus notes in this respect

two (at least apparent) paradoxes: on the one hand, thought, containing all the adequate ideas of all things whose essence follows from *all* their attributes, seems thus 'to extend itself much more widely than the other attributes'; on the other hand, singular things, as modes of substance, seem to have to be 'expressed in infinite ways' (that is, to derive simultaneously from an infinity of attributes), while the definition of the human individual centred on the soul as 'idea of the Body' seems to mean that the essence of a singular thing includes only one mode of thought and one mode of another determinate attribute. (Letters 63, 64, 65, 70, 72)
3. Finally, how does the (lone) attribute of infinite extension carry out the deduction (and, correspondingly, production) of the *existence* of singular things, conceived as 'parts' of matter or of the 'Body', having a determinate figure and motion? (Letters 69, 70, 80–3)

All these questions have in common the implication of new relationships between *infinity* (of substance, of each attribute and of the effects which follow from a cause or an essence), *causality* (of substance, of infinite extension in itself and of the modes between them – indeed, this is Tschirnhaus's 'counter-sense' of the object of an idea of this idea) and finally the real *singularity* (of essences and existences). They also reflect the confusion of Spinoza's reader at his rejection of the traditional depiction of the 'possible' and of the 'real', reinscribing all thought of the possible into the order of the real instead, either in the form of the anticipation of its actualisation, or that of the logical universe from which it derives the conditions of its existence.

But two aporias cannot fail to strike us in this exchange of arguments (which was interrupted, albeit by death). When

Spinoza is asked to clarify the way in which, from the causal definition of a *real thing*, an infinity of properties or consequences arises, he gives as an 'example' *the definition of God*, while the point of difficulty obviously lies in *singular things* (Letter 83). In particular, when he was asked by Tschirnhaus (who thought he had found the promising beginnings of a physics in Part II of the *Ethics*) to explain how the existence of extended modes is deduced (or constructed) from the essence of their attribute, Spinoza begins by dodging the question, reiterating his critique of the Cartesian 'geometric' conception of extended matter, both quantitative and inert. But he finally confesses that on this question he has 'not been able to set out anything concerning them in an orderly way': in short, he has not managed to prove anything (Letters 81 and 83).

Should we be wary of this confession? In relation to the classic duality of Descartes's geometric mechanism versus Leibniz's dynamism (which correspond to the directions explored by Tschirnhaus, who is trying to find in each mode or real individuality an expressive infinity which, implicitly, identifies it again with substance), Spinoza seems to be searching for a third way or for a way around. But, in this context at least, he does not manage to explicate this other than in a general manner. We find here the aporia of Spinozist physics (and of his philosophy qua metaphysics), as anticipated in his letters to Boyle and Oldenburg, before the elaboration of the *Ethics*. The difficulty is represented by the multiplicity of existing things, apt to 'compose' – or to 'agree' in forming – real 'wholes' and 'parts' (this is the 'configuration of the whole Universe': *facies totius universi*), although their essences only express modes of a single substance. We find, moreover, that this can be read simultaneously on two levels. It bears on the individuality of singular things, conceived both as the essence and as the *effect* of universal causal 'connection', and it bears on the meaning and epistemological function of the concept of the attribute, since that represents both an essence from which an infinity of other essences can be deduced, and an existence constituted by the infinite chain of all the given existences that can affect one another.

The dilemma is thus renewed: either an ontology that is coherent in itself, but not 'fit' for founding a physics, or an enigmatic juxtaposition of ontology with a theory of the body, that we perhaps find in effect again at each major turn of Spinoza's system. Gueroult proffers this latter interpretation, believing that 'the *Ethics* must be based on physics as much as on metaphysics',[8] but also concluding that a problem in the unification of the different concepts of 'cause' persists in Spinoza's account of immanence.[9] This leads him to deem there to be *two* 'physics' in Spinoza: one, 'abstract' and 'purely relational', involves the study of the constitution of individuals as modes of extension, and would in fact be a variant of mechanism excluding any finality; the other. 'concrete', expressing a 'metaphysical substratum', takes us 'into the interior of things', where their *conatus* communicates directly with the unity of substance – the necessity for this move being indicated by the impossibility of applying to the 'supreme individual, namely the whole universe' the schema of the pressure of surrounding things.[10] By contrast, Negri considers that Spinozist being, first determined as unequivocal in the terrain of ontology, 'on the terrain of knowledge . . . is presented as equivocal being': this is why 'the tension that is released here . . . can therefore be resolved only on the terrain of practice'.[11] He sees the system evolve from a utopia of being as plenitude towards an 'ontology of the' practical constitution of the real, in which 'the infinite is not organised as an object but as a subject',[12] which is to say, as the power (*puissance*) of the multitude and the multiplicity of powers, of the 'productive forces' organising themselves collectively, tending towards their liberation.[13] In the *Ethics*, Negri sees us passing from one metaphysics to another, the index of this passage being the progressive 'extinction' of the concept of the *attribute*, the last trace of the metaphysics of emanation.[14]

Let us try to reopen this question, *without* admitting as obvious the terms 'physics' and 'metaphysics'.

## The Two Ways of Producing Singular Things and the Plurality of 'Worlds'

The correspondence with Tschirnhaus, despite the incomprehension of one of the interlocutors and the exit of the other, shows the possibility of understanding the relationship of substance, attributes and modes according to two antithetical patterns, each of which represents the beginning of quite a different ontology.

Either – this is what I will call path A – the concept of substance is 'distributed' across an infinity of distinct attributes, which each expresses its essence in its own way, which is to say that all of them are equally substantial. And it is these attributes that are *then* affected by finite or infinite modifications, which ultimately results in things which are 'singular', both in their essence and in their existence. Singular things are thus produced from substance *via the mediation* of attributes, in accordance with their own essences and causalities. Singular things are thus represented as being 'in' (or 'of') substance through the mediation of the attributes that are themselves already 'in' (or 'of') substance. This is seen as being unavoidable, because they have nothing in 'common', except the very substance which they express and which we know through them. Singular things therefore have a kind of 'double' singularity: insofar as they differ from one another 'modally' (which does not mean abstractly or fictitiously), and insofar as they differ from the modes of all the other attributes. For example, an idea is different from any other idea *and* from any body. Or indeed a determinate relation of motion and of rest, characteristic of a corporeal individual, differs from any other equally determinate relation, *and* differs from any idea (including the idea *of the* body that it forms, which is to say from its 'soul').

But a mediation is also a separation: the modal difference, redoubled by the attributive difference (by the allocation of things to the 'field' of a determinate attribute, be that thought, extension or something else), ensures the difference of all the modes (including, of course, the infinite modes) from substance itself, and separates the essence and existence of the modes from the essence and existence of substance, and of caused being from causing being.

If we reverse this proposition, we get what I will call path B, by which particular things will be thought as *modes of substance*, without any 'intermediary', because there is no power that produces modes other than substance itself, no ontological difference between the being of modes and the being of substance (which is *their* being). This amounts to saying that the tension between the one and the multiple, the indivisible and the divisible, the immutable and the changeable, and the infinite and the finite is entirely contained in this shift or 'transition' from substance to modes as it occurs 'within' substance itself.

While, as we have seen, path A's logic is to privilege the infinite modes to produce an additional mediation between substance 'specified' by its attributes and singular things or individuals, path B's logic is to consider *the finite modes* to be the 'real' modes, the inherence of which in substance best demonstrates the originality of Spinozism, as opposed to any doctrine that makes the finite a degradation of the infinite, or a reality 'intermediate between the infinite and the void' (as Descartes was led to write). This is why the way in which each finite mode 'involves' infinity is here the decisive problem of ontology.

In these terms, what does the concept of attribute mean or, rather, what purpose does it serve? How can we make it *immediately* intelligible, while allowing that it can be understood in an infinite number of ways? Each attribute constitutes one way, itself singular, of comprehending the inherence of modes of substance. In other words, it is a way of thinking the multiplication (or reduction) of the indivisible and, correspondingly, the shared essence of a multiplicity of absolutely distinct essences. Each attribute, by being 'conceived through itself' (*Ethics* Part I, Proposition 10), just like substance itself, and by 'expressing an eternal and infinite essence' (Proposition 11), thus *negates* for us, by the same token, any distance between modes and substance. In other words, it does not appear to be a mediation, but an immediately given *unity of opposites*. Thus, infinite extension (or the infinity of extension) makes it possible to think the unity of an infinity of singular things as a 'body' admitting or denying other bodies; infinite thought (or the infinity of thought) makes it possible to think the substantial unity of an infinity of singular things as 'ideas' linked in a chain with other ideas that affirm or negate them. But the difference between attributes *is not added* to the difference between modes: to say that an idea 'differs' from another idea in the same sense as it 'differs' from a body – whether we understand this abstractly or transcendentally – would be an absurdity. This effectively leads us to think that singular things, each defined by its essence or its cause, should, just like substance itself and because they are only its effects, be thought according to its infinity of attributes (the infinity of 'infinities').

Within the understanding that our intellect can have of it, every thing conceived as a body must be joined with an idea of the same thing, in other words 'its soul' (*omnia sunt animata*). But this understanding cannot exhaust either the infinity of substance or that of the modes. From this perspective, the 'finitude' of the human individual would be marked from the start by the fact that it only ever perceives a portion of the attributes of substance, which is to say that it only perceives singular things under certain attributes (in fact, two). One cannot conclude from this that it is barred from any adequate knowledge of things, or even that it is 'missing' anything, since knowledge of things is nothing other than knowledge of causes and this is adequate no matter what attributes come into play.

Reciprocally, we must suppose that every idea is essentially the soul of something, which can be conceived as a body, or otherwise. This, however, is what Spinoza seems to reject explicitly in Letter 66 to Tschirnhaus, instead introducing the difficult idea of an *infinity of souls*, 'expressions' of each thing in the infinite intellect of God, which is not found in the *Ethics* (at least I have not found it there).[15]

Is this alternative really Spinozist? Nothing is less certain. It is clear, however, that in this form, or forms close to it, it is at work in the divergent readings of Spinoza, whose mutual incompatibility never ceases to amaze. Path A seems to lend itself particularly well to a mechanistic reading, in which each attribute represents an infinite multiplicity of its kind, sufficient to explain a kind of chain of causes or reasons. For example, the order and connection of things insofar as they are modes of extension or of bodies is entirely intelligible as the 'external' composition of movements, the 'pressure from surrounding things' (Gueroult) etc.[16] Analogously, the order and connection of ideas as modes of thought would be intelligible as a 'logical space' of their relations of composition. Conversely, path B inevitably suggests that the reality of things is *still beyond* what each numerical multiplicity expresses, so that it corresponds to a 'internal' infinity. It lends itself naturally to a vitalist or energeticist reading. Who would claim that the interpretation of the *conatus* of essences, in particular, has never escaped these dilemmas?

Each of the two paths actually leads to its own line of interpretation of the fundamental categories. Each highlights, by the obstacles it comes up against, the strategic functioning of certain statements of Spinoza's, but also the difficulty of reconciling them on a first reading.

On path A, substance acts in fact only by its attributes, hence the temptation to 'substantialise' these. Does Spinoza not use expressions like 'each being must be conceived under some attribute' (*Ethics* Part I, Proposition 10, Scholium), 'modes of each attribute' (primarily Part I, Proposition 25, Corollary; and Part II, Proposition 26; but also Part I, Propositions 21–3; Part I, Proposition 28, Definition; Part II, Proposition 5, Definition; Part II, Proposition 7, Definition), 'corporeal substance' (actually, only in the introductory part of the *Ethics*;[17] Part I, Proposition 13, Corollary; Part I, Proposition 15, Scholium; and in the correspondence)? In the complete definition of God, what makes him substance 'consisting of an infinity of attributes each of which expresses an eternal and infinite essence' and what becomes primary and essential is, then, the infinity (qua infinite power) *of each attribute*. As for the fact that substance

(God) 'possesses' an infinity of attributes, or rather consists of infinite attributes in an infinity of ways (bearing in mind the classic difficulty of translating the word *constans*: 'constituted by' or 'consisting of'), it is difficult not to perceive it as secondary, superimposed on the main idea. This is already clearly indicated in the distinction of the two attributes we can name, that is to say, precisely the minimum required to formulate such an idea, unless we are tempted to view that as the form in which Spinoza is perpetuating the theological idea of an eminent divine perfection, of a being 'infinitely more real' than anything of which our finite intellect may have an idea.

It is no longer, then, attributes whose function might seem evanescent or formal. It is substance itself. What, then, is the point of substance? I think it can be seen in the shift from an epistemological point of view to an ontological point of view. The autonomy of the attributes raises a problem of their 'correspondence', without which no objectively true knowledge would be possible. Proposition 7 of Part II will in its turn affirm the reality of this correspondence, in the form of a strict reciprocity. And substance will then be the 'foundation' of this correspondence, in the sense of an always already acquired guarantee. But this also, it must be said, produces a mystery. For substance to ensure the correspondence of two given attributes, it is indeed necessary that it 'includes' them in a superior reality that 'precedes' them. It is here that the infinity of infinites that defines substance (almost a contradiction in terms!) becomes operative. But this infinity of infinites is a mystery to us – paradoxically, since it is what founds the possibility of knowledge. One can imagine all too well some opponent here turning against Spinoza his expression 'sanctuary of ignorance'. And they would not be off the mark.

Thus, we would discover in Spinoza a surprising analogy with both Descartes and Kant. There is an analogy with Descartes since the guarantee of the objectivity of ideas shifts from divine truth to the productivity of substance, from the 'creation of eternal truths' to the substantial unity of the attributes, but without losing, in fact, its arbitrariness: on the contrary, it is no longer just about our understanding of the divine guarantee, but would belong to God-substance, always being removed from its expressions. There is also an analogy with Kant insofar as the 'schematism of the transcendental imagination', the foundation of the correspondence between the conditions of the possibility of experience and those of the objects of experience themselves, remains a 'hidden art' in Kant. But what is not a problem for Kant (since it is for him precisely a matter of establishing the impossibility of a knowledge of things in themselves and the inherent limitations of pure reason) would raise a serious difficulty for Spinoza, who never ceased (against Descartes) to maintain that making the infinite unknowable would render all human knowledge impossible.

All this can be put differently. Spinoza thinks the 'correspondence' between attributes as the identity of the causal *connections* in each of the attributes. On path A, this identity will be built step by step, treading always in conformity with the nature of the attributes. The first, decisive step will be the 'correspondence' between *the infinite modes* of different attributes (*Ethics* Part I, Propositions 21–3; Letter 64); this is to say, first of all, between the infinite immediate modes, namely the universality of motion on the one hand and the idea of God in his own infinite intellect on the other, which is to say between two systems of 'eternal truths', which can be interpreted as the 'laws of nature' (extension) and the 'laws of thought' respectively. Then, taking a further step, correspondence would be established between the mediate infinite modes: the *facies totius universi* and the ensemble of all ideas, which are both part of the *natura naturata*. Finally, the last step would be correspondence between 'parts' of the extended universe and 'parts' of the complex (or complexes) of ideas, including singular things. The complete structure of this correspondence would express the identity of the causal order of things with the rational order of ideas.

But there must in turn be a cause of this sequence. If substance is this cause, it will be the 'cause of causes'. This is compatible with the idea of God being 'absolutely the first cause' (Part I, Proposition 16, Corollary 3), but less compatible with the idea of God as 'the immanent, not the transitive, cause of all things . . . which are in him' (Part I, Proposition 18) and still less with the idea that 'God must be called the cause of all things in the same sense [eo sensu] *in which* he is called the cause of himself' (Part I, Proposition 25, Scholium) and that 'God cannot properly be called the remote cause of singular things' (Part I, Proposition 28, Scholium), in other words that there is no difference of reality between the effects of divine causality, whether infinite or finite. As might be expected, the representation of substance as cause of the attributes, themselves cause of the modes (or of attributes as super-modes of substance, themselves the object of a 'second' modification), is the impasse of path A.[18]

Let us return then to path B. Here, the modes are modes of substance itself, without intermediaries, and, unlike on the path just described, *the infinity of attributes* will take on a fundamental importance, which first of all overcomes the fact each attribute is itself 'infinite in its kind', or, rather, which cannot be separated from this. From the outset, this infinity excludes, as inadequate to the essence of substance, the enumeration of attributes, and even their denomination by exclusive terms, which can only represent, at best, an 'auxiliary of the imagination' (Letter 12). But what, positively, is the infinity of attributes, if it is not a mystery but a concept or an essence?

Let us re-read Propositions 16–18 of Part I, which deal explicitly with the infinity of attributes: 'From the necessity of the divine nature there must follow infinitely many things in infinitely many modes [infinita infinitis modis] (i.e., everything which can fall under an infinite intellect)'. So 'there can be nothing outside him [God] by which he is determined or compelled to act'. Thus God 'is the immanent, not the transitive cause of all things', that is to say, he is the cause 'from the laws of his nature alone' of 'things, which are in him' and, conversely, 'outside God, nothing that is in itself can be given'. These are quasi-axiomatic propositions (Part I, Proposition 16, 'must be plain to anyone'), which imply that divine power has no limitation (not even any 'self-limitation', the habitual recourse of theologies of the emanation) and therefore *no externality*. It acts entirely by itself. In short, the idea of infinite attributes first entails the theory of immanence, with its fundamental asymmetry: the essence of the modes is different from that of substance (since they are not infinitely infinite), but substance does not exist elsewhere than its modes, neither in a physical or intellectual 'other place', nor, as according to the mystics, in a withdrawal of Being, a primordial nothingness, or some absolute 'other' of all beings.

Yet, if substance acts *only in itself*, without ever externalising itself, it does necessarily *act* in itself. The difficulty is how to think effectively, in a conceptual or definitive way, this action or this production of effects from which finite things and all their mutual ('transitive') actions result *as* the realisation of infinite divine power. This is precisely the focus of the famous Proposition 7 of Part II, 'The order and connection of ideas is the same as the order and connection of things' (ordo et connexio idearum idem est ac ordo et connexio rerum), when interpreted from the point of view of the infinity of attributes.

Again, Spinoza himself points out that this is an almost axiomatic statement. The tradition presents it as positing a 'parallelism' of attributes (a term Spinoza never used). In reality, Proposition 7 of Part II does not come, after the fact, to confer an epistemologically remarkable property on *already given* attributes. It does not follow the distinctions between them, but puts their use in order. If one thinks to read here the designation of two exemplary attributes, it is by a retrospective illusion, from being trapped in metaphysical and epistemological dualisms, one which Spinoza, at this precise point, proposes to suppress once and for all. Insufficient attention is paid to the fact that, in this statement, there is no question of scope, or of juxtaposed attributes, but of 'things' that can be thought under any attribute (*including* infinite thought itself) and of 'ideas', which is to say of the intrinsic adequation of ideas to things, on condition that the one and the other are thoughts *as causes* (as indicated elsewhere by the variant *ordo et connexio causarum* – Part II, Proposition 7, Scholium).

But this adequation immediately brings us back to the infinity of substance. Between 'the order and connection of things' and 'the order and connection of ideas', there can be no question of *correspondence*, in the sense that the 'elements' of two sets ('things' or 'ideas') would correspond term by term and would maintain homologous relationships between them. It is not a matter of overlaying a table of ideas onto a table of things, to depict the causality of one by that of the other. Exactly what Proposition 7 of Part II says is that there is an identity of order-and-connection, that this 'is the same' (*idem*) and not something else (different or differing), that is, that there is *a single reality* to be thought as 'order-and-connection'. Reciprocally, the same or identical can be thought in its reality only as 'order-and-connection' (and not as an isolated event). This reality can therefore only be *substance itself, insofar as it is identical with the cause*. The practically indecomposable expression *ordo et connexio* (which I would suggest here be translated as 'order *of* connection', exploiting a classic figure of Latin grammar) signifies the essence of substance; not, however, the way the initial definition (as self-caused, existing by itself and conceived by itself) did, namely in a way that was still nominal and abstract. But synthetically, the exposition of Part I makes it possible by the end to understand the identity *all* the senses of the concept of 'cause' within the activity immanent to infinite power, or, which amounts to the same thing, the internal complexity of the cause. Therefore the Demonstration of Proposition 7 of Part II can be presented by Spinoza as an *alternative formulation* of Axiom 4 of Part I: 'The knowledge of an effect depends on, and involves [eamdem involvit], the knowledge of its cause'.

This alternative formulation makes it possible to remove the ambiguity of the expression *causa sui*, which always risked being understood as the application 'to itself' of a transitive concept of causality (or as the reflexivity of a 'relation' $x \, R \, y$, in positing $x = y$), and leading to it being elevated to the status of the first cause or to it being extracted from the complex of causes. But it also rules out singular things appearing to us as the simple phenomena of things in themselves just as much. The infinity of attributes *positively* expresses this double negation. It posits the self-identity of the necessary connection of an infinity of singularities or differences. Substance thus appears as the power of individuation, the productive cause of *its* modes because it causes *itself* in causing *them* in a unique way, as causes *of one another*.

Now, an adequate idea of this power does exist. 'Attributes express the essence of substance'; each one of them 'expresses the reality, *or* being [realitatem sive esse] of substance' (Part I, Proposition 10, Scholium): without it being necessary to compare it with others, it realises the order of connection of *all* the modes of substance. But each one of them expresses, in its own infinity, the infinity of all the others. No adequate idea (being realised itself as an order of connection, which is to say necessarily producing the series of its own effects) could therefore introduce a gap in reality or a break in principle between knowledge and its object. If, by a hypothesis which is a fiction, 'things' were not 'causes' realising the very causality of substance, they would not be knowable in the causality of ideas. Conversely, in things there is nothing else to know than singularities determined by a unique power to cause and be caused.

Does this mean that path B, as I have just outlined it, does not involve any difficulty? Obviously not. The first is that, from this perspective, instead of substantialising attributes, we might be tempted to 'de-realise' them, by considering them to be mere conceptual 'points of view' on substance. In the most extreme form of such a reading – which would be another way to read Kant into Spinoza – attributes would become like transcendental forms delimiting the *a priori* conditions *under* which the causal essence of substance and its modes can be conceived by a subject. This temptation conflicts with Spinoza's opening statement that the essence of substance is being 'conceived through itself'. And above all, it contradicts what we have just stated: that the infinity of each attribute is indissociable from the collective infinity of attributes and the attribute is even infinite in an identical sense. This temptation cannot therefore amount to a point of view or a restriction.

But if the identity of an infinity of attributes expresses the fact that the same causal necessity, included in the essence of substance, produces 'things' and 'ideas', another difficulty arises. In Spinozist ontology, things and ideas (which are themselves things) must be conceived immediately as causes. Yet Spinoza maintains a distinction between *essences* and *existences* (except precisely for the case of substance itself). It seems, then, that the split between things and ideas is going to be deferred to the level of the difference between essences and existences. We know that essences are absolutely positive and cannot be negated by each other. This is why, notably, the false and the true do not reciprocally destroy one another: 'Nothing positive which a false idea has is removed by the presence of the true', as they each adequately express some essence, that is to say, they are each the idea of a modification of divine power. But while certain existences are compatible with one another, others mutually destroy one another, which means that they cannot 'be in the same subject' (Part III, Propositions 4 and 5). This is why Spinoza ignores any problematic of 'compossibles' or the 'compatibility of essences', and transfers the principle of contradiction from the domain of essences to that *of existences.*[19]

To account for this difference, which is at serious risk of turning into a chasm, it would seem we will have to 'split' causal necessity again. Can the notion of an attribute, without equivocation, be transferred from the causality of the essences, wherein singular objects are inscribed into an infinite series of equally positive essences, to the order of existences, where 'force relations' are established between particular causes *with unequal power*, acting on each other to preserve, alter or destroy one another? Should we not admit here the pure and simple irrationality of this point? This could be the meaning of the (lone) Axiom of Part IV (which of course must apply to all attributes, including when the 'thing' of which it speaks is an existing idea), a fundamental axiom for ethics in which we move from power as cause to power as natural law: 'There is no singular thing in Nature than which there is not another more powerful and stronger. Whatever one is given, there is another more powerful by which the first can be destroyed.'

However, the positivity of essences and the conflict of existences are both required in order to think the power proper to singular things, or the *conatus* by which they 'seek' to persevere in their being. Every singular thing or, better still, every real individual is thus conceived as a point (or moment) of identification of the order of essences with the order of existences. On the other hand, in the *totality* of each infinite attribute, and even in the totality of the modes thought under this attribute (for example the *facies totius universi*, which is also an individual, eternally identical to itself), power relations coincide with an essential interiority, understood 'from the perspective of eternity' (sub specie aeterni). At these two levels we find something like the immediate presence of substance. But, as Tschirnhaus sensed, we remain unable to explain what connects each individual to this infinite totality as one of its own 'parts'.

In short, the schema of the two paths allows us to highlight a knot of interdependent difficulties. Is there a totally unified concept of causality in Spinoza, encompassing in an intelligible way the very production of singular things and their interactions, capable of being expressed equally in terms of 'laws of nature' and 'laws of thought'? Or should we assume that real causality is only thinkable specific to different 'kinds of existence' that would represent attributes – their common inherence to substance then being responsible to account both for the necessity of all causal chains and for the equality between them (so that no form of causal necessity can be considered the 'model' for the others)?

Is the individuality of things a kind of 'by-product' of their modal existence, always already thought *under* determinate attributes? This would mean the difficulty would then be to understand what confers a singular *essence* on each individual, and not just a natural *form* that is relatively stable under certain conditions. Or should we consider the singularity of modes to be a direct expression of divine power (which, we have seen, can be thought in the strongest sense as the power of individuation)? This would then make the difficulty one of not conferring on individual essences the status of archetypes, and correlatively on existences a participation in the essences for which the attributes provide a sort of 'material'.

Formally, these questions recapitulate the classic dilemmas of philosophy. They make one wonder whether the Spinozist concepts of substance, attribute and mode lend themselves indefinitely to ambiguity, or whether, on the contrary, their strange articulation is not the 'solution' found by Spinoza to the antinomies of metaphysics, a solution which, paradoxically, in the very words of metaphysics, demands that we leave them behind. The impression of an ambiguity would then amount very simply, disarticulating the Spinozist demonstration, to continuing to project anew onto its concepts assumptions that Spinoza considers imaginary and wants to leave behind, be they those of an anthropology (the persistent trace of which appears

## INDIVIDUALITY, CAUSALITY, SUBSTANCE

in the problem of the 'correspondence' of attributes), or those of a theology (which always pushes us to reverse the positivity of substance into the negativity of a principle which is not something it can itself determine).

To grasp what Spinoza means, at least three conditions seem to be required.

The first is not surreptitiously to re-establish the distinction between the *possible* and the *real*, and the antecedence of the former over the latter. The 'two paths', separated from one another, are both attempts of this type, one starting from the distinction between the infinite and the finite, the other from the distinction between essence and existence.

The second is, as Pierre Macherey underlines in a recent book,[20] to take seriously the thesis of the infinity of the infinite attributes themselves, that is to say, to avoid reinscribing this in the space of a numerical multiplicity, including understanding the thesis of the *uniqueness* of substance as a numerical predicate, which is to say as the negation of a plurality. One is reminded here of Wittgenstein's proposal: 'Logical forms are without *number*. Hence there are no pre-eminent numbers in logic, and hence there is no possibility of philosophical monism or dualism, etc.'[21] The 'number' of attributes has no essential signification; or, rather, 'going beyond number', it immediately signifies that, if we are compelled by the logic of contradiction to say that substance is *one,* we cannot understand by this that it is *nothing but one.* However impractical this may be in practice (how can we inscribe *one* in the discursivity of a demonstration, and simply in logic, without reducing it to *nothing but one*?), this thesis must be the red line for our reading.

The third condition is to apply an analogous interpretation to the *individuality* of singular things. At the antipodes of the idea of a *species infima*, of an atom or individual substance, germane to cosmological classifications and hierarchies, the uniqueness of Spinozist individuals means they are neither irreducible *vis-à-vis* others, nor marked by interiority as opposed to exteriority, but, rather, are the adequation of a thing to its own essence, which is its power to act or be a cause. This is why this singularity implies no incompatibility with the idea of 'common notions', even though it is incompatible with their use as abstractions. This is the paradox of Spinoza's 'nominalism', which affirms the idea of necessary connections instead of dissolving it.

These conditions are problematic, but they bring out the stakes of the problem. At base, Tschirnhaus's quandary was already a very good indication of this. At one point he supposes that there 'must be as many worlds established as there are attributes of God' (Letter 63), which is to say a world of extension, *plus* a world of thought, *plus* even more worlds, on to infinity. At another, he postulates that 'the world is unique' (Letter 65), from which he concludes that there must be an infinity of different expressions of one and the same modification which are like many points of view on the reality of the thing. The appearance of the two paths (the ambiguity of substance) can be seen clearly here to be linked to *our* need to represent nature as a 'world' of things (which can also be of people, more or less stable states, etc.) and things as things for a 'world', their existence as a 'being in the world', whether it is a matter of a world for man, or of a world for God.

Conversely, if Spinoza's thought (with its idiosyncratic notions of 'the whole of Nature forming one single Individual' and of the 'order of Nature', but also of man as 'part of Nature') corresponds to neither of these paths exactly, does it not represent an attempt to think a Nature that is not a World – even an infinite World, thus escaping any 'conception of the world'? This time I would be wrong to cite Wittgenstein: 'To view the world *sub specie aeterni* is to view it as a whole – a limited whole. Feeling the world as a limited whole – it is this that is mystical'.[22] Rather, I will go back to Althusser: the effort to think 'causality, which would account for the action of the Whole on its parts, and of the parts on the Whole', makes Spinoza the 'first and almost unique guide' to the thought of 'an unbounded Whole'.[23]

## Notes

1. *Ethics* Part II, Proposition 38.
2. Letter 32, Curley translation – the bracketed gloss is Curley's, and conveys information included in Balibar's original French.
3. *Descartes' Principles of Philosophy*, Part II, 36.
4. *Ethics* Part II, Lemma 7, Scholium. In his own work, *Descartes' Principles of Philosophy* (Part II, Propositions 12, 13, 15), Spinoza summarises the position of Descartes, who makes God the (sole) cause of the creation and preservation of 'motion and of rest'. However, we can note: (1) that he omits to specify that this quantity is conserved, as Descartes said, 'in the universe'; and (2) that this exhibition (with Part I, Axion 10, to which it refers, and therefore also Part I, Proposition 7) gives rise on his part to the maximum 'theological' interrogation and objection. This point should be examined closely from the perspective of a reading of *Descartes' Principles of Philosophy* as a laboratory of a Cartesian logic. Gueroult discusses Spinoza's attitude in relation to the Cartesian principle and concludes, 'here the problem of the internal coherence of Spinozist physics is posed', and further on, 'we must admit that Spinoza allowed incompatible doctrines to be compresent in his physics'. Martial Gueroult, *Spinoza, Volume II* (Hildesheim: Georg Olms Verlag, 1974), pp. 179–81, 563–9.
5. Do not forget, though it changes nothing, that this formula is from Saint Thomas, for whom it plays an essential role in the definition of truth starting from the 'science of God': 'Unde unaquaequae res dicitur vera absolute secundum ordinem ad intellectum a quo dependet' (*Summa Theologica*, I, Quaest. XVI, art. 1).

6 See, for example, Eugene P. Wigner, *Symmetries and Reflections* (Woodbridge: Ox Bow Press, 1979). When Newton has to account for the remarkable simplicity of Kepler's laws, that is, for the *visible* harmony of the solar system, he must assume initial conditions specially created by God, logically independent of the physical laws themselves. It is difficult to distinguish this idea from that of a miracle.

7 Of course, it is necessary to ask to what extent this dilemma is replicated when Spinoza himself proposes to constitute (in the *Political Treatise*) a 'science' or theory of political individuals, that is to say of the causes of the fluctuation of states and their mode of 'regulation'.

8 Gueroult, *Spinoza, Volume II*, p. 145.

9 Martial Gueroult, *Spinoza, Volume I* (Hildesheim: Georg Olms Verlag, 1968), pp. 409–12.

10 Gueroult, *Spinoza, Volume II*, pp. 145–89.

11 Antonio Negri, *The Savage Anomaly: The Power of Spinoza's Metaphysics and Politics*, (Minneapolis: University of Minnesota Press, 1991), p. 43.

12 Ibid., p. 166.

13 Ibid., pp. 183ff.

14 Ibid., pp. 46, 59–62, 189–90, 213, etc.

15 The puzzle is this: God thinks each thing (or there is in God an idea of each thing) according to an infinity of attributes while 'we' only think according to two attributes. But in so doing God thinks 'nothing more' than us, as long as we have an adequate idea. It is surprising that Gueroult does not examine Letter 66 when he discusses 'an at-first-insurmountable objection to the assertion that there are as many different souls as correlative modes of the Body [sic] in the infinity of other attributes' (Gueroult, *Spinoza, Volume II*, pp. 255–6). For his part, Negri (*The Savage Anomaly*, p. 190 and note 10) writes, 'certainly . . . in discussions with Tschirnhaus . . . Spinoza clarifies the critique of the attribute and of any possible emanationist reading of the system. . . . However, there are still many ambiguous points in these letters regarding the conception of the attributes. Spinoza seems to have a certain fidelity to the totality of his "written" system, to the totality of his work, even while he is in the process of developing alternative avenues.'

16 It seems to me doubtful that, in this regard, the possibility of discovering in Spinoza the anticipation of a physics of 'fields' of forces – see Jonathan Bennett, *A Study of Spinoza's Ethics* (Cambridge: Hackett, 1984), pp. 88ff. – changes any aspect of the problem, especially since it is accompanied by the explicit thesis that *there are only two attributes* of substance that really matter.

17 That is to say, in the process of construction of the indivisible substance, which is at the same time the process of deconstruction of the Cartesian duality of substances, of which his terminology necessarily bears the trace.
18 Note that Descartes explicitly posits 'modes' and 'attributes' as species of the same logical genus, which is, according to the Aristotelian tradition, the attribution of properties to a subject: the name of attribute is reserved for primary, essential properties; that of modes (= modes of modes or attributes of attributes) for secondary, contingent properties (*Descartes' Principles of Philosophy* Part I, 56).
19 See Gilles Deleuze, *Expressionism in Philosophy: Spinoza* (New York: Zone, 1990), pp. 192ff; and Pierre Macherey, *Hegel or Spinoza* (Minneapolis: University of Minnesota Press, 2011), pp. 170ff.
20 Macherey, *Hegel or Spinoza*, pp. 95ff.
21 *Tractatus*, 4.128.
22 Ibid., 6.45.
23 Louis Althusser, *Essays in Self-Criticism* (London: NLB, 1976), p. 141.

# 2

# Individuality and Transindividuality in Spinoza

Before justifying the title of this chapter and indicating the source of the terminology I have used, please allow me some preliminary considerations which will serve to explain what I feel to be the issue at stake.

In the past, many philosophers (albeit not all of them) have explicitly addressed the problem of the *essence of man* (to which Aristotle had proposed a double solution: man by nature is a 'speaking animal' and a 'political animal'). Some have rephrased the biblical exclamation 'What is man?' (*quid est homo, quod memor es ejus?*; Psalm 8: 5) as a speculative or transcendental question. Some have combined the two in order to develop a 'philosophical anthropology' (a term which, of course, was introduced later). In this history Spinoza has a remarkable position, both because of the pivotal role which the question of 'essence' plays in his main work and because of the eccentric answer he gives in response. Part III of the *Ethics*, as we know, virtually begins with a construction of the essence of man (which in many respects parallels the construction of the essence of God in Part I) leading to the famous phrase in the Scholium of Proposition 9: 'Hic conatus . . . cum ad Mentem et Corpus simul refertur, vocatur Appetitus, qui proinde nihil aliud est, quam ipsa hominis essentia, ex cujus natura ea, quae ipsius conservationi inserviunt, necessaria sequuntur' (When this striving . . . is related to Mind and Body together, it is called Appetite. This Appetite, therefore, is nothing else but the very essence of man, from whose nature there necessarily follow those things that promote his preservation). This same Part ends with a variation of the formula, at the beginning of the first Definition of the Affects, incorporating the precision which initially had been postponed: 'Cupiditas est ipsa hominis essentia, quatenus ex data quacunque ejus affectione determinata concipitur ad aliquid agendum' (Desire is man's very essence, insofar as it is conceived to be determined, from any given affection of it, to do anything). In between, there has been a full development of the anthropological theory. This is precisely what allows us to take these formulas not only as nominal definitions of appetite and desire, but also as real definitions of the essence of man.[1]

The full circle which seems to be traced in Part III is also remarkable because it allows us to transform an abstract, merely generic understanding of the essence of man (which is the way Proposition 9 and its Scholium must be read, if only because they appear as an application of the propositions which concern the *conatus* or *actualis essentia* of any thing), into an adequate knowledge of *the individual's essence*. The Demonstration of Proposition 57 repeats the formula in this way: 'At Cupiditas est ipsa uniuscujusque natura seu essentia . . . ergo uniuscujusque individui Cupiditas a Cupiditate alterius tantum discrepat, quantum natura seu essentia unius ab essentia alterius differt (But desire is the very nature or essence of each [individual]. . . . Therefore the Desire of each individual differs from the Desire of another as much as the nature, *or* essence, of the one differs from the essence of the other). The metaphysical notion of essence has thus undergone a profound change (already illustrating the transition from the Second to the Third Kind of Knowledge): instead of referring to a class or a genus, it now refers (as a result of the theory of the affections, in which Desire is the prime mover) to the singularity of individuals. It is a principle, not of unification, but of determination or differentiation. That the essence of man is equated with *cupiditas* becomes all the more provocative from a religious point of view, since the singularity or *ecceitas* of each individual is precisely what a theological world-view would address while speaking of *quod sit homo*. But to such a world-view *cupiditas* would bear a direct relationship with mortal sin, and therefore refer to an alienated aspect of the human essence.[2]

At this point, it seems to me worthwhile to look at the role played by the terms 'consciousness' and 'determination' in Spinoza's definitions. Even though he rarely uses the word *conscientia*, it is nevertheless most significant. It appears only three times in the *Ethics*, all of them in Part III: in the Scholium of Proposition 9 ('inter Appetitum et Cupiditatem nulla est differentia, nisi quod cupiditas ad homines plerumque referatur, quatenus sui appetitus sunt conscii et propterea sic definiri potest, *nempe Cupiditas est appetitus cum ejusdem conscientia*' [between appetite and desire there is no difference, except that desire is generally related to men insofar as they are conscious of their appetite. So *desire* can be defined as *appetite together with consciousness of the appetite*]); in the Demonstration of Proposition 30 ('Laetitia cum conscientia sui tanquam causa afficietur' [Joy, together with a consciousness of himself as the cause]); and in Scholium 2 of Proposition 18 ('Conscientiae morsus' [Remorse]), which we cannot exclude as long as we are not certain that, for Spinoza, the 'moral' and 'psychological' meanings of *conscientia* are distinct (a distinction which, in the very same period, in English led to the emergence of the word 'consciousness' in addition to the already existing 'conscience').[3]

Clearly, the Scholium of Proposition 9 is the most important occurrence. It is closely related to the way Spinoza uses *conscius* or *sui conscius esse* in other passages (where most of the time the idea that men are 'conscious of their appetites' or 'their wills' goes along with the idea that they 'ignore the causes' which make them act one way or another, therefore perpetuating the illusion of free will). But this is not a *definition* of 'consciousness'. Indeed, this definition is never provided by Spinoza. I suggest that we reverse the question, considering the Scholium of Proposition 9 and related formulas an *implicit definition of* conscientia *or 'consciousness'*. Given that Spinoza provides us with a detailed description of the forms, causes and effects of desire (*cupiditas*), we may consider, in his theory, *'consciousness' to be nothing else but the (modal) difference between Appetite and Desire,* which is typically human. That is, the difference between the 'effort' or *conatus* to preserve itself for the human individual as a whole (*cum ad Mentem et Corpus simul refertur*) and the basic *affection* which, combined with Joy and Sadness, Hate and Love, Hope and Fear, give their emotional value or polarity to our relationship with any object.

With this in mind, what are we to make of the words 'ex data affectione determinari ad aliquid agendum' (to be determined to act, or do something, by some affection)? I take it to be a very general formula in which all the processes of transition between passivity and activity are included, inasmuch as they are *causal* processes. Since the 'effect' which is indicated is an action, there is a clear suggestion here that, although individuals (especially human individuals) are both passive *and* active, the natural tendency of an individual's existence is towards activity. This also means that emotions are always referred to this basic orientation. Precisely this dynamic difference or *momentum* is reflected in 'consciousness', or it takes the form of an individual's desires.

This makes it fairly difficult to understand, it would seem to me, the kind of criticism which, again and again, has been hurled at Spinoza's anthropology, namely (1) that he was unable to give an account of *subjectivity* (in other words, he was an adamant behaviourist or reductionist), and (2) he was unable to give an account of the individual's *autonomy* (the only 'proper' individual in his conception ultimately being 'God', i.e. a total, impersonal and undifferentiated entity). This kind of criticism began soon after Spinoza's doctrine became known. However, in my opinion, such criticisms are not rooted only in ignorance or bad faith. They ultimately refer to the intrinsic difficulty which readers had (and still have) in understanding a doctrine which virtually escapes (or dismisses) the basic antinomies of metaphysics and ethics which arise from ontological dualism: individualism versus holism (or organicism), but also the opposite ways of understanding the human 'community' itself, in which either 'intersubjectivity' or 'civil society', 'interiority' or 'exteriority', is given primacy.[4]

***

Since Alexandre Matheron's landmark book, *Individu et communauté chez Spinoza* (1969), which one could say is in a sense entirely dedicated to making this point, we have known that Spinoza's philosophy is essentially irreducible to the standard dualisms of the history of ideas, in particular that of individualism versus organicism (or holism, as we now say, using the Anglo-Saxon terminology), but also that of social relations conceived as exteriority (according to the model of the *Gesellschaft* or 'civil society', as it is understood from Locke to Hegel, starting from an essentially legal problematic) versus as interiority (according to the model of the *Gemeinschaft* or constituent intersubjectivity).[5] We know that this irreducibility represents not just one consequence of Spinozist philosophy among others, but, rather, the basis of his theory of finite modes and their natural production. In other words, it highlights the most central intention of the theory which, in Spinoza, takes the place of ontology (or, rather, forms the Spinozist alternative to ontology, allowing that exactly contemporaneously, ontology is finding itself refounded as first philosophy, at the very same time that it is finally given the name 'ontology' as such).

Discussing the 'foundations of interhuman passionate life' in the third part of the *Ethics*, Matheron attaches particular importance to the logic of affective imitation and especially to the effects of the *ambition for glory*, which inspires in individuals the desire to behave and to conform in order to do what they imagine would please those whom they perceive as their fellows. In this, he tells us, 'the very foundation of sociability is discovered'. And he adds:

> Such a feeling, if it brings the exaltation of the ego to its peak, is not, however, 'interested' in the ordinary sense of the term. It does not imply that we regard others as a means; it is not based on any calculation, contrary to what Hobbes believes. . . . If we want to please men, it is not to be able to use them later; this will happen, of course, but secondarily. And nonetheless this ambition is not 'altruistic' in the Comtean sense either. It is located beneath these alternatives, in an original locus where

egoism and 'altruism' coincide: to rejoice, without utilitarian thought, in the joy that I give to my fellows is *the same thing* as to love myself through the love they show me.[6]

Later on, Matheron takes up the same theme again, this time in relation to the 'foundations of reasonable life' as they are set out in Part IV of the *Ethics*. He forges, somehow out of traces in Spinoza's text, a remarkable *oxymoron*: 'we arrive, at the end of this first stage' of the genesis of relations of mutual utility, as 'interhuman consequences of our essential desire' for preservation, 'at what could be called a biological *ego-altruism*'.[7] In the final reckoning, as the two demonstrations of Proposition 37 of Part IV show, 'rational imitation' corresponds to 'passionate imitation' and it reveals the latter's necessity:

> We thus find, in a de-alienated form, all that was positive about the affections studied in group B1 of book III. Certainly pity and envy are irretrievable as such, because Reason is never sad and its Sovereign Good is shareable. But ambition remains, ... the *ego* and the *alter* being assimilated to one another, we are now beyond the egoism-altruism opposition: this is symmetrical to the passionate ambition which is found on this side.[8]

The *opposition* of 'selfishness' and 'altruism' *therefore never exists*, in the strong sense of the term (except in a state of nature which Matheron shows is only a limit concept, and in no way reducible to the isolation of individuals, which would make it impossible for them to survive). It is only an inadequate representation, engendered by passionate life, but incapable of explaining its essence.

Would it not be appropriate, then, to seek to overcome any conceptual duality and, following Matheron's lead, to seek, in the way in which Spinozist individuality is constructed, an ontology (or meontology) of relation and communication, of which forms of moral and political life, imaginary as well as rational, simply form the actualisation? This is what I would like to sketch here by extending some previous attempts. It seems to me that this means combining three key ideas.

In the first place, individuality is not only a central notion in Spinoza, but the very form of necessary – and consequently real – existence. In a strong sense of the term, *only individuals exist*. The individual is obviously not a 'substance', as in Aristotle, but conversely substance (or God, or Nature) does not 'precede' individuals: it is nothing *other* than their multiplicity. It designates in the same way the infinite process of production of individuals and the infinity of causal connections existing between them.[9]

Secondly, an individual is a unity: any real individuality is composed of distinct parts ('atoms' or *corpora simplicissima* are therefore not individuals, and do not have any separate existence).[10] Above all, individuals are given neither as a 'subject' nor as separate matter, nor as a 'form' organising matter, nor as a 'compound' of matter and form following an end or a model, but the effects or moments of a process of individuation and, indissociably, of individualisation. These two aspects are necessarily united in what Spinoza calls *natura naturans*. The passage from *natura naturans* to *natura naturata*, which is the very essence of causality, consists precisely in this twofold process, which individualises modes by individuating them.[11]

Hence, thirdly, the fact that the construction and activity of individuals originarily involve a relationship to other individuals. No individual is in himself 'complete' or self-sufficient: if each individual becomes (and remains, for a certain time at least) a singular unity, it is because *other* individuals also become and remain singular units. In other words, the *processes* that make individuals relatively autonomous or separate are not themselves separate, but reciprocal or interdependent. This interdependence goes far beyond the distinction between individuality and environment or milieu, between 'inside' and 'outside'; rather, it reformulates this in terms of interaction between real individualities. It is another name for necessity, or for the negation of contingency, as stated in Proposition 29 of Part I, which must be construed in a strong sense: if it is true that 'in rerum natura nullum datur contingen: sed omnia ex necessitate divinae naturae determinata sunt ad certo modo existendum et operandum', then 'nothing', that is, no individuality, can be connected to others solely *a posteriori* or from 'outside'. It is to the very extent that all natural production leads to individualities that tend to increase their degree of autonomy as far as possible (or to act 'adequately'; cf. *Ethics* Part III, Definition 2) that the very idea of processes of individuation being isolated from one another becomes unthinkable.[12]

The consequences of this point of view become apparent when it is revealed that the *conatus* of each essence, by which it *affirms* itself, implies at the same time a resistance to its destruction by other 'contrary' things and a combination or coalition with other 'similar' things against adversity. All alterity is, in a sense, a threat, but against this threat there is no recourse other than alterity, or reversing it into agreement. In the historical and political field, *conatus* is called the 'natural right' of each thing, and the simultaneous criticism of individualism and organicism is expressed in the double fundamental demonstration: the autonomy or power of individuals is not reduced, but increased, by the constitution of civil society or the state; the sovereignty or power of the state is not restricted, but increased, by the autonomy of individuals, especially their freedom of thought and speech.

One sees why a logic (shall we say a dialectic?) of *coincidentia oppositorum* or, better yet, of *simultaneous rejection* of abstract opposites is required here. If it is necessary to give a single positive term to this, the best one seems to me to be *transindividuality*, as used by Simondon in his posthumous book, *L'individuation psychique et collective*.[13] The convergence of these analyses is all the more remarkable given that Simondon denies any debt to Spinoza, whom, in a rather conventional way, he sees a 'pantheistic' philosopher negating individuality as such. My objective here is not, however, to explore this convergence in detail, but to ask to what extent Spinoza himself can be considered as a theoretician of the transindividual *from* the first propositions of his 'ontology' (which, significantly, he calls an 'ethics'). His philosophy would thus help us to go beyond purely negative formulations (neither individualism nor organicism, but neither mechanism nor finalism either) to arrive at a constructive concept, with an undeniable actuality. For this we need to make sure that the *Ethics* enunciates a definition of individuality as transindividuality, or, better yet, as a process of transindividual individua(lisa)tion.[14]

I will try to do this by cursively re-examining some of the major problems of Spinoza's œuvre. I will begin with the problem of the *schema of causality* outlined in Parts I and II of the *Ethics*. Having shown that this must be understood in terms of reciprocal action 'modifying' or 'modulating' the expression of singular essences, I will proceed to the construction of successive *orders of individuality* (as defined in Part II, which gives the premises of the anthropology of Parts III and IV), in other words the question of the integration of (relatively) 'simple' individualities into (more) 'complex' individualities. I will then discuss the possibility of understanding in the same terms the articulation in Parts III and IV of the concepts of imagination and reason. This is, in other words, the relationship between the psychological laws of imaginary life on the one hand, which Spinoza derives from the original ambivalence of human desire, and on the other the rational rule of reciprocal utility, from which the possibility of establishing relatively stable political communities proceeds. Finally, I will comment on Part V, re-reading it from this perspective.[15]

## The Spinozist Schema of Causality

In the first part of the *Ethics*, transindividuality first appears as a *schema of causality*. This expression with its Kantian resonance seems to me to characterise – within the set of Propositions 26–9 that, for the first time, actually identify 'God' and 'nature' – the proper object of Proposition 28:

> Quodcumque singulare, sive quaevis res, quae finita est, et determinatam habet existentiam, non potest existere, nec ad operandum determinari, nisi ad existendum et operandum determinetur ab alia causa, quae etiam finita est et determinatam habet existentiam: et rursus haec causa non potest etiam existere, neque ad operandum determinari, nisi ab alia, quae etiam finita est et determinatam habet existentiam, determinetur ad existendum et operandum, et sic in infinitum.[16]

Like each schema, this is both a logical concept and a representation. It ascribes to the relations of cause and effect a topology of which we can immediately identify the two characteristic traits.

First, this topology is non-linear – the interaction of a multiplicity of terms is not derived from it – but originary, always already involved in the 'elementary structure' of causal action. The schema of causality is not therefore, as it is in Kant, a *succession*, but from the outset a *Wechselwirkung*, which is to say a reciprocal action or interaction. Or alternatively, what is 'elementary' is always already complex. Secondly, the 'order of connection' (*ordo et connexio* or *concatenatio*) which constitutes it is not established between atomic terms (whether objects, events or phenomena) but between *res singulares*, which, in fact, are always individuals.

That the Spinozist schema is non-linear – this being its precise difference *vis-à-vis* the Kantian schema[17] – is evidenced by the very way in which Spinoza defines a 'modification' (a finite mode of the nature of God), constantly employing his characteristic expression 'ad existendum et [aliquid] operandum determinari'. In the Demonstration of Proposition 28, Spinoza identifies a 'cause' and a (finite) 'mode' – 'Deinde haec rursus causa, sive hic modus debuit etiam determinari ab alia' – and in the last Proposition (36) of Part I ('Nihil existit, ex cujus natura aliquis effectus non sequatur'), he closes the circle opened by Axioms 3 and 4, by showing that every natural thing is a 'cause', and that there can be no cause that does not produce any effects.[18] From the perspective of the infinite productivity of substance, *existence* and *operation* are in fact synonymous notions:[19] to exist means to operate or act on other things. But this operation itself is always necessarily determined by some *other* thing or cause. Consequently, 'causing' is the operation by which something modifies (or 'modulates', as Simondon says, borrowing from the vocabulary of signalling theory) the way something else operates (or produces its effects). This is why the infinite connection of causes cannot be represented by an addition of independent linear series, or genealogies of causes and effects (A 'causes' B, which 'causes' C, which etc.), but only by an infinite network of singular modulations,[20] or by a dynamic unity of both modulating and modulated activities (the modulating action of B on the operation of some A is modulated by the action of some Cs, itself modulated by the action of some Ds, etc.). In other words, the elementary schema cannot be represented like this:

$$A \to B \to C$$

but rather only like this:[21]

$$A \searrow \underset{B}{\swarrow} C$$

If it is necessary for these singularities to be individuals, it is precisely because only they can be said to be *modified in order to modify*, which Spinoza expresses by saying again that they are *affected in order to affect*. That is why, in a strict sense, only individuals 'act' or 'operate'. Note here that, throughout the *Ethics*, Spinoza uses the terms *afficere*, *affectio* and *affectus* as connected notions with an unvarying signification, which express the essence of God in (or according to) his different attributes ('Res particulares nihil sunt, nisi Dei attributorum affectiones, sive modi, quibus Dei attributa certo et determinato modo exprimuntur').[22] This will justify Spinoza's claim that he has been able to account for the human passions without having introduced the slightest 'exception' into nature. And let us note already the homology of the definitions of causality in general and of the general definition of desire insofar as it is 'the essence of man' (that is, of *every* human singularity, according to his own multiple variations): 'Cupiditas est ipsa hominis essentia, quatenus ex data quacunque ejus affectione determinata concipitur ad aliquid agendum'.[23] The essence of causality is indeed a 'differential' of activity and passivity within the same 'subject' or – as Spinoza prefers to say – the same individual, but it is precisely this unity that is expressed in each individual's *conatus* by binding him by the same token to an infinite multiplicity of other individuals.[24]

The comparison with Kant could again be very significant here. Both thinkers have only one general schema for explaining the order of physical causes and the order of moral or 'practical' effects: in Kant, it is that of temporal succession; for Spinoza, that of modulation.[25] But Spinoza's schema does not attempt to oppose the two levels of reality, making one the mirror image of the other. Whereas in Kant a causal order is a linear *ex post* determination, and a final order is a linear *ex ante* determination, operating by means of anticipations or intentions (that is, representations of goals), Spinoza makes 'practice' a modulation in the same way as any operation, or as any individual causality; freedom thus becomes not the *reversal* of the natural order, but the necessary expression of its active side. The whole question of the structure of time is also thereby altered.[26]

## Transindividual Integration

However, such a description only paints part of the picture. It only introduces a 'first order' complexity into the elementary schema of causality, by establishing an equivalence, or – as mathematicians might say – a duality between the idea of each individual's existence or activity and the idea of multiple connections between different individuals. In a strong sense, each individual qua an existing mode is the set of conditions of its existence, given within an infinity of other individuals.[27] Proposition 7 of Part II of the *Ethics* calls this first order of complexity the 'same order' of connection, displayed in the same way in things as in ideas. But the propositions that follow immediately after this introduce a second order, which allows us to specify our common notion of nature as involving the concept of the individual as a determinate level of *integration*, incorporating other individuals ('lower' levels of integration) and incorporated in its turn, with the others, in 'higher' levels of integration. It is here, it seems to me, that the very notion of the individual expands to include the *process of individua(lisa)tion*, the transindividual dimension of which is irreducible.

Of course, the idea of an individual being composed of 'parts' which can in turn be part of the composition of more general 'wholes' is nothing original. It is this, moreover, which gives rise to the classical antinomies that correspond to the fact that one or the other term is posited as prior to the other (individualism and organicism, mechanical and organic unity, etc.). In Letter 32, Spinoza takes up this point again to demonstrate that, in nature, there are *objective* orders of magnitude, which are associated with reciprocal actions or interactions ('omnia enim corpora ab aliis circumcinguuntur, et ab invicem determinantur ad existendum et operandum certa ac determinata ratione').[28] The distinction between the 'whole' and 'parts' appears to be relative: what is a part at one level becomes a whole at another, and vice versa. But this does not imply that the levels themselves are arbitrary: they are based on the existence of the 'same ratio of movement and rest' between the parts of each unity which retains its shape or remains stable (as far as it does) – 'certa ac determinata ratione, servata semper in omnibus simul, hoc est, in toto universo eadem ratione motus ad quietem', an idea in Descartes's 'laws of nature' that Spinoza has taken up, but in order to turn it back against its original creationist context and apply it not to the 'world' but to the singularity of *each particular level* of integration.[29] In Spinoza, a 'constant ratio of motion and rest' can exist at different levels (and no doubt at an infinity of levels, even if only some of them are known to us and practically concern us), which means that relatively autonomous bodies, stable or stabilised for a certain time, really exist (as long as this 'ratio' is maintained), contrary to what happens in Descartes, where the 'law' applies only to extended substance considered in its totality. Consequently (as the lemmas after Proposition 13 of Part II explain), for each individual its identity (the fact that it remains 'the same', and therefore 'itself') is explained by a constant ratio at a determinate level. But its variations or transformations are explained by the constancy of a ratio at a *different* level.

Such a presentation, however, although referring to 'dynamic' concepts (of ratios of movement and rest), is nonetheless dependent on a static – and, ultimately, finalistic - representation of nature, conceived as a hierarchy of forms, or as a general order of the subsumption of individuals within one another, according to their degree of complexity (or of the multiplicity of their elements). This defect comes from the fact that we always come back to what Spinoza calls *natura naturata*, in which the 'individual' is a formal notion that applies indifferently to all levels of integration (the representation of the whole of nature as 'one individual' come from precisely this point of view), as if this natured nature, as a hierarchical order given between two limits, from the *corpora simplicissima* to the *facies totius universi*, was the result to which the 'naturing' power tends as its end. But the small 'physical treatise' after Proposition 13 contains another idea of causality, expressed in Postulates 3–6. It concerns precisely the way in which an individual body is affected by others outside it. In the demonstrations of Propositions 19 and 24, it becomes very clear that the doctrine expounded is not a physics in the restrictive sense of laws of motion, but a theory of the very nature of 'things' or 'individuals', expressed in the attribute of extension just as well as it might be in any other. It is this that will allow Spinoza, without any break in continuity, to call the *conatus* of the essence, in Part III, the same 'constant ratio of motion and rest', an effort to persevere in its existence, which, for each finite mode, makes it a component of the infinite power of nature or *natura naturans*.[30]

What does Spinoza actually say? That each individual's preservation, that is to say its stability and identity, must be compatible with a 'continuous regeneration' of its parts, what today we would call a regulated inward and outward flow. Materially, it is constituted by a continual exchange with other individuals. Mentally, it is constituted by the fact that all consciousness of the body mixes up or 'confuses' its own states with ideas of other things, just as the perception of external objects is mixed up or confused with a representation of the body itself.[31] To say that an individual continues to exist is simply to say that it is regenerated or reproduced. An isolated individual, deprived of exchanges with the other individuals that form its environment, could not be regenerated. It would not exist. And therefore Spinoza implies from the outset that every individual needs other individuals to maintain its form and existence (see Postulate 4 of Part II and his use in the proof of Proposition 39 of Part IV: 'Quae efficiunt, ut motus, et quietis ratio, quam corporis humani partes ad invicem habent, conservetur, bona sunt; et ea contra mala, quae efficiunt, ut corporis humani partes aliam ad invicem motus, et quietis habeant rationem').[32]

Of course, to say that the exchange is 'regulated' means that it results from a relation between forces (*potentiae*), and that it involves destructive as well as constructive effects which must find an equilibrium. Now, it is not enough to suppose here that the exchange takes place 'between' different individuals: it is necessary to specify *what is exchanged*. On this point Spinoza expounds a simple but daring idea: it is the *parts* of the individual itself. 'Regeneration' means that a given individual (who may be called *ego*, or, better yet, *se* or *seipsum*; one encounters this phrasing in politics in the formulation *sui juris esse*, which means, strictly speaking, since right is power – *esse suae potentiae*) constantly abandons certain parts of itself, while constantly incorporating some parts from others (which one can call *alteri*), on the condition that this substitution leaves some invariant 'ratio' or essence.[33] Now it is clear that the *ego* or *seipsum* thus preserves its essence if the dynamic ratio that defines the individual is itself preserved, independently of whether or not others' essential ratios are preserved. Clearly, 'my' preservation may very well involve 'their' destruction. But the opposite is also true: the entire process can be viewed from the point of view of any of the individuals involved; 'their' preservation may very well imply 'my' destruction.

Such an explanation, if at least it does not distort Spinoza's doctrine, nevertheless raises problems. How, in particular, can a regulatory process understood in this sense admit of degrees? When Spinoza describes human life, he tends to posit a radical alternative to preservation and destruction, in an all-or-nothing logic that leads to the definition of an 'enlarged' concept of death as the discontinuity or rupture of memory (cf. Proposition 39 of Part IV and its famous Scholium of the 'Spanish poet').[34] Yet the very notion of an 'increase' or a 'decrease' in an individual's 'power to act', resulting in an increase or decrease in its autonomy, seems to imply that there are degrees of *conatus* or *margins of variation* between individuals' indefinite preservation and immediate destruction. It is also difficult to explain what rules, or what circumstances, make the preservation of a given individual compatible or incompatible with that of other individuals (hence, from the subjective point of view of an *ego*, make 'my' preservation compatible with 'theirs').

But does this difficulty not provide the programme of subsequent parts of the *Ethics*, at least for the case of human individuals?[35] It seems to me that its solution must be sought in the implications of Spinoza's model of the construction of the individual (or of individua[lisa]tion) according to an originarily transindividual causality. The demonstration of Proposition 24 of Part II shows that, to be able to exchange parts with others, each individual must undergo a *virtual decomposition* (which, of course, applies to 'me' as well as to 'others', in short to 'everyone' – *unusquisque*). In other words, when certain parts of an individual are acted upon by external things, it is because they are cut off or simply isolated from the set to which they belong, forming a transitory unity with certain parts of other individuals. In Spinozist terms, one can say that they are then considered not for their contribution to the initial individual's essence or internal ratio, but as separate individualities which can be subsumed under other *rationes*. What Spinoza is saying is that any individual who acts on others and suffers by others' actions (the two being necessarily linked) is somehow placed 'outside himself', but that one must not conceive this interaction as a 'one-on-one' confrontation between indivisible individuals. Individuals mutually modify each other or 'mingle' with one another because they exchange constituent parts (which are always material, but one can of course understand this to mean not only extended parts, but also signals), or because they are constantly 'analysed' and 'synthesised', decomposing into more basic parts and recomposed into relatively autonomous units.[36]

It is, then, apt to ask what distinguishes a virtual decomposition, which is transitional or reversible, from an actual, irreversible decomposition, which is to say from the destruction of an individual.[37] The answer to this question is given to us by Spinoza in the theory of social relations in Part IV: it deals with human individualities, but he takes care in his demonstrations not to rely on common notions. Everything depends, in fact, on the single Axiom of this Part: 'Nulla res singularis in rerum Natura datur, qua potentior et fortior non detur alia. Sed quacunque data datur alia potentior, a qua illa data potest destrui'.[38] The more complex an individual is, the more relations it will have with the outside world, the more intense the exchange of 'parts' with other similar or dissimilar individuals will be, and the more necessary they will be to preserve its own existence, but also the more its own preservation will be threatened by the superior power of the very things it needs. I therefore understand Spinoza's thesis, in the final analysis, to be that the *multiplicity* of other singular things is necessarily stronger, more powerful (and potentially more destructive) than any particular singular thing ('me' or the 'self'), all the more so because all these things form a unity or a set from which 'I' am excluded. On the other hand, the strength of any given finite multiplicity of external (opposing) things is always likely to be surpassed by a set or 'combination of forces' (a *convenientia*) of which 'I' would myself be a necessary part (which is to say, the characteristic ratio of motion and rest of which I enter into). In the last instance, this process is endless, and could go on to encompass the whole of *natura*, which is to say that the *perspective* of integration and of collective augmentation of power could go on to infinity. This means that this process has no end.[39]

In Propositions 2–7 of Part IV, Spinoza describes the play of partial causes, hence the necessary role of passivity in the preservation of human individuals. Passivity is the superiority of external causes, the virtual decomposition of the individual. It is inevitable. But any affection can be repressed (*coerceri*) by a contrary affection. This idea is presented, first of all in a general way in Propositions 29–31 of Part II (which give a general description of the effects of *convenientiae* on the preservation of individuals), and then applied to the human case in Propositions 38–40 (after the presentation of society as a system of reciprocal utilities). The relationships that are established between individuals by virtue of their 'common nature' form a collective or 'superior' individuality *without*, however, suppressing their autonomy. On the contrary, they increase their *potentia agendi* (including their ability to think and know), and therefore their power to exist.[40] If we remember the Axiom of Part IV (the natural superiority of external forces), we can conclude from this that the unification of a multiplicity of individuals through their mutual 'conveniences' is an intrinsic condition maintaining its autonomy ('individuation') and its singularity ('individualisation') for each one of them. If the individual could not find other ones with which it 'agrees' to regenerate it, it simply would not exist.[41]

We can therefore finally conclude that the complete concept of an individual represents an equilibrium, not fixed but dynamic, which would be immediately destroyed if it were not continuously reconstituted. Such an equilibrium (which, following Simondon, we could call *metastable*) implies that in the process of virtual decomposition or deconstruction a process of recomposition or reconstruction is permanently superimposed. Now, even though this represents nothing but the singular essence of the individual (although it is exactly what Spinoza calls its *conatus*), it is determined in its very essence by 'collective' processes, that is to say, 'constant ratios of movement and rest' or *convenientiae* which incorporate the individual into a greater individual, or into an individual of a 'higher' order.

This is why I have suggested that the Spinozist theory of natural causality has a 'second-order' complexity, in addition to the first-order complexity expressed in Part I, Proposition 28, and summarised in the formula *ordo et connexio causarum*. It is not just about interaction or about a reciprocity of causes situated 'at the same level', but about the process of interaction which, for each type of individual (*individuorum genus*, in the terminology of Lemma 7 after Proposition 13 of Part II), regresses to the lower, underlying level, and *simultaneously* progresses to the higher, encompassing level.[42] Clearly, Spinoza thinks this schema is universal – that is why it can be explained in 'common notions' – and that it underlies all natural causality (which means that the 'first order' of complexity that expresses a static connection between individuals always comes from the second, which represents the collective equilibrium of partial decompositions and recompositions). However, this explanation can be given fully only when we think of the individuals who come into play as human beings. No doubt this is because, in that case, we can draw the necessary elements from our experience (*Experientia sive praxis*, as the *Political Treatise* 1.3 says). But what experience?

Precisely that of the conflicting affections which influence our degree of activity or passivity, which make us oscillate between increasing and decreasing independence with regard to partial causes: experience of the harmonious or conflictual unity that we form with other things, and especially with other men. Experience, in this sense, of existence itself, not as opposed to reason, but as always already including it.[43]

## 'Society', or the Transindividual Mediation Between Imagination and Reason

At this point, several objections may occur to readers of the *Ethics*, based in particular on Spinoza's distinction between 'adequate' causes and 'inadequate' causes, and more precisely between being a cause inadequately (being primarily passive, determined by external causes) and being a cause adequately (being primarily active or producing effects explained 'by our own nature'). This is generally understood by contrasting situations where we depend on other individuals with those where we are independent and act 'by ourselves'. Now, the reasoning I have outlined above suggests that Spinoza should be interpreted in a much less 'individualistic' way: to be active, or an 'adequate cause' of one's own actions, is *also* to establish a relationship with other individuals, but one that should be thought in terms of *convenientia* or synergy and not of 'dependence', even as 'mutual'.

Such an interpretation is certainly not obvious, but I believe that it can be defended and I would now like to do so. One could certainly begin by suggesting that when Spinoza speaks of man or human nature (as in the *Ethics* Part IV, Proposition 4: 'Fieri non potest, ut homo non sit Naturae pars, et ut nullas possit pati mutationes, nisi quae per solam suam naturam possint intelligi, quarumque adaequata sit causa')[44] he is not necessarily referring to a single individual, but employing a generic expression. This defence, however, would be rather a fragile one, because it is forced in its phrasing, and because Spinoza, throughout his demonstrations in Part I, is careful to distinguish between what concerns individual (or personal) affections and what is a collective or collectivising process. Now, it is not a question of suggesting that the idea of transindividuality erases this distinction: as I understand it, it is no less opposed to organicism than to atomistic individualism. We must therefore have recourse to a stronger, but also trickier, hypothesis. Note that Spinoza *never* says, when speaking of actions of an individual that can be explained by his own or unique nature (*per solam suam naturam intelligi*), that this individual acts alone or in isolation. To draw this conclusion would precisely imply 'individualistic' postulates, begging the question. Furthermore, one may note that the 'model of human nature' (exemplar humanae naturae) of which the Preface of Part IV of the *Ethics* speaks in fact excludes any individual perfection which would depend on *the isolation* of man (including of the 'free' man or of the 'wise man'). On the contrary, it associates perfection (or, it would be better to say, *perfecting*) with the idea of a growing autonomy of the individual (in the double sense of a growth in freedom and in singularity) which goes together with growth in 'friendship', which is to say with ever closer association with other individuals. This, it seems to me, is the way chosen by Spinoza in his treatment of the relations between imagination and reason in Parts III and IV to articulate their individual and collective aspects.

Let us start from the famous criticism of 'humanism' (in the sense of affirming human nature to be something unique and miraculous, outside the common laws of nature) that appears in the Preface to Part III: 'Imo hominem in Natura veluti imperium in imperio concipere videntur'. The sentences immediately following make it clear that this amounts to arguing not only for the same rational method to be applied in the science of man as with other natural beings, or that human nature depends on ordinary causality, but also for explaining human behaviour in terms of interactions with other natural beings, human or not. This follows logically from the fact that man (or 'human nature') is not *outside* nature (either as its 'master' or as its 'beneficiary'), and leads directly on to the statement of definitions and postulates of this Part, which associate the distinction between activity and passivity, and thus the definition of affects in terms of increasing or decreasing the power to act, with the different modalities (notably temporal) of the relation of the body to external objects.[45] This statement is all the more remarkable because Spinoza – I repeat – does not intend to proceed in Parts III and IV to dissolve or reduce individual identity, especially with regard to human individuals. He proposes to reconstruct this identity, by synthesising all the determinations of this identity, or by producing what we could call a complete 'phenomenology'.

Spinoza begins with the question of *consciousness*, which he conceives of as an idea of the 'self' qua body and mind, affirming the existence of its 'object' (*ideatum*). This is why consciousness is always associated with desire. But this is only an abstract starting point. The full description of self-consciousness can only arise from a complete (natural) history of desire, in other words of the passions and actions involved (which may be modalities, consequences, or causes of its metamorphoses). It will be a history of singular units, combining each time ideas and affects, and mixing images of present or past objects with perceptions of oneself, making the self into a concrete reality or making individuation into a process of individualisation. If it is necessary to admit that such a process necessarily involves a transindividual dimension from the outset, it will have to be manifested at the heart of the logic of desire, the very principle of the association of ideas with affects. However, from the outset, Spinoza also *subdivides* his object by introducing the basic distinction between *passions and actions*, or between 'inadequate' and 'adequate' ideas, imagination and reason. This amounts to claiming that – logically at least – the *mens* of the individual is divided, *split* into two sets of ideas, or that the unity of its 'consciousness' is always uneven and divided in itself. We must therefore begin by taking up separately the question of the transindividual constitution of the imagination and that of the transindividual constitution of reason, as if they were two heterogeneous forms of mental life, before attempting to reconstitute the synthesis into a single process.

Let us start with the imagination. And let us be careful not to project onto Spinoza's text arguments inspired by later psycho-sociological or psychoanalytic theorisations, as tempting and useful as those rapprochements may appear.[46] Nevertheless, Spinoza's theory of the imagination is not an enumerative theory of the *faculties* of the mind or of human nature generically conceived (memory, perception, will, imagination, etc.) but, rather, takes as its object the very *structure* of the constitution and differentiation of the individual 'self', including self-awareness as well as self-identification or self-recognition and self-assertion. This theory describes this structure in terms of originally transindividual relations: it does not only, in fact, confront us with a conception of consciousness in which any relationship that 'I' can establish with 'myself' would be mediated by the Other (or, more precisely, by an image of the Other), but shows the life of the imagination to be a circular process of successive identifications, in which I never cease to imagine the Other via my image, and to imagine myself via the image of the Other. One might be tempted to think that this way of conceiving the structure of the imagination represents a secularisation and a generalisation of the biblical maxim (which we know Spinoza considered the core of the 'true religion' of which the *Theological Political Treatise* speaks): 'Thou shalt love thy neighbour as thyself', except that Spinoza also introduces in this transposition the idea of the inherently *ambivalent* character of passions and processes of identification, which involve not only love but also hatred.

Propositions 15–17 of Part III occupy a crucial place in the explanation of how the life of the imagination gives rise to what I have called a 'history of the self'. They show the genesis of an internal conflict in which mutually opposed affects (above all love and hatred) derive for a given subject from its relation to one and the same objects ('Haec Mentis constitutio, quae scilicet ex duobus contrariis affectibus oritur, Animi vocatur Fluctuatio, quae proinde affectum respicit, ut dubitatio imaginationem').[47] This ambivalence will be overcome only by the introduction of temporal modalities of joy and sadness (hope and fear), which will only add a new intensity to the oscillations of passionate desire. It is also remarkable that these propositions refer explicitly to the idea of an individuality composed of multiple parts that can be associated with others by so many 'partial' causes and thus be affected simultaneously in multiple ways. The key concept here is that of the *aliquid simile*, or partial 'likeness', by way of which an individual associates joy or sadness with the images of other individuals, arousing in himself feelings of hatred or of love towards them and arousing his own desire to please or displease them: 'Ex eo solo, quod rem aliquam aliquid habere imaginamur objecto, quod Mentem Laetitia, vel Tristitia afficere solet, quamvis id, in quo res objecto est similis, non sit horum affectuum causa, eam tamen amabimus, vel odio habebimus'.[48] Spinoza describes the whole imagination as a kind of mimetic process.

The following section examines the consequences, in order to introduce another crucial concept, that of the *affectum imitatio*: 'Ex eo, quod rem nobis similem, et quam nullo affectu prosecuti sumus, aliquo affectu affici imaginamur, eo ipso simili afficimur'.[49] The relationship to the other is therefore a double process of identification: we identify with other individuals because we perceive a partial resemblance between them and us (that is, a resemblance between *parts* of the body or mind, which become positive or negative objects of desire) and we project our own affections onto them at the same time as we do theirs onto ourselves.[50] Hence the continuous circulation or communication of affects between individuals, which is also the process in which each individual's affections are reinforced. In this collective and personal Janus-faced process, collective 'identities' are constituted along with individual ones. We try to imitate others and act according to the image we have made of them, and we try to get them to imitate us and act according to the image we project from ourselves onto them.[51] But this is also a 'translation' of the process we described above as one of de-composition/re-composition into the language of the mind or psyche. From this we can also hypothesise that Spinoza was already trying to prepare such an analysis of the problem of personal and collective identities when he described the preservation of the individual as a process which necessarily also implies *infra-individual* and *supra-individual* levels.

Imagination is therefore a transindividual reality consisting of mimetic processes of partial transfer of ideas and of affects. But what of reason? It is introduced in the Scholium of Proposition 40 of Part II as a 'Second Kind of Knowledge', in which thought is governed by *common notions*. These are common in the double sense that they apply universally to any object and that they belong to all human minds, qua ideas of properties that exist both in the whole and in the parts. No doubt such 'common notions' can relate to ethical as well as to theoretical matters. It may even be necessary to go so far as to postulate – recalling what was said above about the possibility of thinking *common notions* as *convenientiae* – that any theoretical axiom should also have an ethical value, just as every rule of action that is universally valid implies a true idea. But the question of reason will not be tackled again until the Scholium of Proposition 18 of Part IV:

> With these few words I have explained the causes of man's lack of power and inconstancy, and why men do not observe the precepts of reason [cur homines rationis praecepta non servent]. Now it remains for me to show what reason prescribes to us, which affects agree with the rules of human reason [quinam affectus cum rationis humanae regulis conveniant], and which, on the other hand, are contrary to those rules [contrarii]. . . . Since reason demands nothing contrary to nature, it demands that everyone love himself, seek his own advantage, what is really useful to him [quod revera utile est], want what will really lead man to a greater perfection [id omne, quod hominem ad majorem perfectionem revera ducit, appetat], and, absolutely, that everyone should strive to preserve his own being as far as he can. . . . Again, from Part II Post. 4 it follows that we can never bring it about that we require nothing outside ourselves to preserve our being, nor that we live without having dealings with things outside us [ut ita vivamus, ut nullum commercium cum rebus, quae extra nos sunt, habeamus]. Moreover, if we

consider our Mind, our intellect would of course be more imperfect if the Mind were alone and did not understand anything except itself [si Mens sola esset, nec quicquam praeter se ipsam intelligeret]. There are, therefore, many things outside us which are useful to us. . . . Of these, we can think of none more excellent [excogitari] than those that agree entirely with our nature. For if, for example, two individuals of entirely the same nature [ejusdem prorsus naturae] are joined to one another, they compose an individual twice as powerful as each one. To man, then, there is nothing more useful than man. Man, I say, can wish for nothing more helpful to the preservation of his being than that all should so agree in all things that the Minds and Bodies of all compose, as it were, one Mind and one Body [quam quod omnes in omnibus ita conveniant, ut omnium Mentes et Corpora unam quasi Mentem, unumque Corpus componant]; that all should strive together, as far as they can, to preserve their being; and that all, together, should seek for themselves the common advantage of all [omnesque simul omnium commune utile sibi quaerant]. . . . These are those dictates of reason which I promised to present briefly here . . . to win, if possible, the attention of those who believe that this principle – that everyone is bound to seek his own advantage – is the foundation, not of virtue and morality, but of immorality.[52]

It seems that we have here the most precise programmatic exposition of a theory of reason or reasonable action. It is not presented as a faculty (and still less as a divine inspiration or a transcendent essence), but again as a structure or system of mutual relations that would make, for each individual, their *conatus* or the effort to preserve their existence imply the knowledge of their own good (*quod sui utile est*) and the establishment of a *commercium* with other men. Each of these three elements is rigorously necessary to the definition of 'reason'.

Spinoza's conception of reason is utilitarian, for two reasons, but in a very specific sense. It is utilitarian firstly insofar as the very principle of virtue for each individual is to seek what is useful to it and what it needs to preserve its *own* existence. Yet (except in very primitive conditions, to which Spinoza alludes in the *Theological Political Treatise*), this is not a question of reciprocal dependency, or not only that. Spinoza is not really interested in the division of labour and the exchange of goods.[53] Let us say, in classical (Aristotelian) terms, that he does not differentiate between the problem of 'life' (*to zên*) and its 'necessity', and the problem of the 'good life' (*to eu zên*). This is because, for him, *knowledge* in general is the condition as well as the result of the effort at preservation. Propositions 26 and 27 reiterate that reason cannot be separated from knowledge, which is its intrinsic power. Reason is therefore 'useful', but not 'instrumental'. It cannot be rational without also being reasonable.

But reason is also utilitarian in the sense that — contrary to any 'Kantian' notion of opposition between the points of view of ends and of means — it prescribes not only reciprocal *utility*, but also the effective *use* by each one of the forces of the other. 'Homini nihil homine utilius': nothing is more useful to a human than another human — nothing, *not even himself.* Each man is not the most useful 'for himself'; rather, it is the other man who is. This allows us to understand why, in the same text in which he defines the maxims of reason, Spinoza shows that the creation of a community constituting, 'as it were' (*quasi*), only one body and one mind, is the pre-requisite for the preservation of each man. It seems to me that we should understand this theory in a strong sense:[54] what makes other humans supremely useful for each of us is not what they *have*, or what they *make* or produce, but what they *are* (that is, their power to act or 'to cause', as individuals, from which what they have, make or produce also derives). It is for the same reason that my usefulness *to them* (and my constant disposition for them to make use of me as a 'means' of their own preservation) is immediately involved in my perception of their utility for me: this is the basis of the concept of friendship.

Proposition 35 (with its Corollaries and its Scholium) develops the reciprocal idea: not only does reason prescribe seeking the common good or common utility through social life ('commerce' in the most general sense), but it actively *produces* this result, which is nothing other than the preservation of existence – 'quatenus homines ex ductu rationis vivunt, eatenus tantum natura semper necessario conveniunt'.[55] If, then, we anticipate what in Part V will be called a community based on intellectual love, for which God is the object – 'plures homines eodem Amoris vinculo cum Deo junctos imaginamur'[56] – we can suggest that such reciprocal use by individuals of one another in society forms the necessary, if not sufficient, condition for the production of common notions, which is to say of adequate ideas which are conceived identically in different minds (*reducing their difference accordingly*). Such ideas require that the minds of which they are *parts* be – to some extent – 'one and the same mind'. Adequate ideas are ideas that allow each of us to know our affections by their causes, and therefore to become active. But these are also ideas that many different individuals 'have' or – to put it better – think identically, and which thus establish a *partial identity* between distinct individuals. Finally, by comparing this kind of identity with the *imaginary identity* (or 'likeness') discussed above – *the image of the Other* as 'alike', 'neighbour' or *alter ego*, from which the necessity to *please* him derives[57] – we can affirm that reason is liberated from this specific form of abstraction which limits the power of imagination (while causing it to proliferate), which explains its ambivalent effects, constructive and destructive. In reason, the other is conceived as essentially useful, not *despite* its singularity or 'individual difference', but because this singularity is a consequence of the general laws of human nature.[58] Consequently, there can be no question of reducing the qualities proper to each individual (his opinions, his way of life, his external appearance) to those of others. This is what differentiates *convenientia* from *similitudo*, 'friendship' from 'ambition', or even 'humanity'.[59] But it must also be said: in drawing this consequence, we are already considering 'reason' not to be a *second*, but also already a *third kind of knowledge*, which posits singularities *as such* as necessary.

Each 'kind of knowledge' can therefore be considered, in its own way, to be a way of establishing the necessary link between the preservation of individuals and the institution of the community. I believe that such a way of reading Spinoza's theory of the relationship of imagination to reason can also help us better understand what the notions of 'passivity' and 'activity' mean for him. Imaginative communication is based on the fact that the minds of individuals are dominated by ideas of similarity that are both inadequate and confused, so they can only oscillate between opposite illusions (believing in the absolute identity or incompatibility of individuals, seeing in humans brothers or natural enemies). As for rational communication, it requires humans to know each other as different individuals who have much in common. 'Under the guidance of reason', men learn that their fellow men are irreducibly singular, since each has what Spinoza calls an *ingenium* of his own, and yet there are more *convenientiae* between them than between all other things. Both cases are indeed ones of transindividuality, which forms the condition of possibility of the existence of individuals, albeit in antithetical ways. Nevertheless, as Spinoza explains in Part IV of the *Ethics*,[60] many of the same effects can be achieved *either* passively *or* actively – which is indeed why there are civil societies or states in which some individuals are passive and others active, or, rather, *every individual* is in his own way to some degree sometimes active and sometimes passive. This is then because of the superimposition of a passive modality and an active modality on the constitution of the same 'social bonds'.[61]

This seems to confirm my hypothesis that the notion of the transindividual designates a process rather than a fixed pattern. What interests Spinoza throughout the second half of the *Ethics* (from Part III onwards) is not describing and classifying 'kinds of life'. There is only one *conatus* and only one problem of the preservation of individuals in nature. Spinoza does not think we can ever eliminate inadequate ideas (which would imply the absurd hypothesis of human individuals freed from the disproportionate power of their environment). Therefore, imagination will necessarily remain part of our mind. But adequate ideas, however little developed they are, are also part of every human mind. If they did not exist, if man were not the cause of any of his actions 'by virtue of his own nature', his affections would immediately lead to his decomposition and death. To think the status of the transindividual completely and concretely is always to consider relations between individuals, or more precisely between parts of bodies and individual minds, as *in transition* from imagination to reason, from a lesser to a greater power to act. This is precisely what Spinoza suggests when he explains that constituting civil societies is a precondition for the freedom of thought and the activity of knowledge. Adding a neologism to the terminology of Spinoza commentary as I do here will probably add nothing to the widely held idea that politics (and especially democratic politics) for Spinoza forms a necessary mediate step on the path to wisdom. But it will better show what is at stake here: such mediation is effective only if it is intrinsic and internal to the 'ethical transition' itself. In other words, it should be possible to demonstrate that, taken literally, another 'kind of knowledge' is also another 'kind of community' (or of communication). I think this is so, but I am not sure that the text of the *Ethics* provides sufficient basis to establish it. The other possibility we have is to consider the *Ethics*, and in particular Part V, as an incomplete, even *aporetic* text, the object of which – in spite of or by means of its 'geometric order', which Spinoza himself sometimes calls 'profuse' ('prolixiori ordine')[62] – is not to construct a system, but to expose the problems and difficulties involved in such an idea. In this sense, Part V would introduce a new modality of *coincidentia oppositorum*, especially inasmuch as it tries to include in the idea of *amor intellectualis Dei* both a greater force of images and affects of love and joy, and a greater number of 'eternal' ideas that transgress the limits of individual minds to become, in this sense, 'impersonal'. And it is from this point of view that the formulation of Proposition 20, already noted above, which directly associates the intellectual love of God and the adequate knowledge of our affections with the *imagination* of as many men as possible, 'eodem Amoris vinculo cum Deo junctos', takes on all its meaning.

## What Is Man? The Transindividual, or the Intersubjective?

Our question therefore remains partly indeterminate, but what makes it interesting to pursue is clear if we compare Spinoza with other philosophers, particularly in the classical age, equally preoccupied with the renewal of the classic (religious and philosophical) question: *What is man?*[63] The most interesting comparison that we can make is with Leibniz. Their starting proximity is indeed as striking as the final opposition of their points of view.

Spinoza and Leibniz were both equally dissatisfied with Cartesian dualism and Hobbesian materialistic atomism. They both sought to derive the conditions for any individual to become more or less 'powerful' or 'autonomous' from nature itself. We find it difficult to fully understand their point of view because the debates of the following centuries (and especially those that developed in the nineteenth century within the 'sociological tradition') have led us to believe that a concept of the individual is stronger or more radical when it is constituted within a more 'individualistic' doctrine. But the opposite is true: we are dealing with a theoretical elaboration of the concept of the individual whose bases, by our criteria, would be considered 'organicist', 'holistic', or profoundly 'anti-individualistic'. Moreover, in the cases of Spinoza and Leibniz, the concept of individuality is extended to nature in general, not restricted to *human* individuality.[64] So you could say they are, paradoxically, highlighting the singularity of the human being by posing the problem of 'individual difference' as a universal ontological problem apt to occur and be expressed in infinitely many modes and to infinitely many degrees in the realm of nature, of which man himself is but a part. However, such a programme can itself be implemented in many ways, and that is why the way naturalism divides into two rival 'naturalisms', which nevertheless have in common that they are in a sense more strongly individualistic than (official) individualism itself, is so interesting.

As Deleuze never tired of saying, Spinoza and Leibniz share a point of view of 'immanence'.[65] An individual can only be singularised by dint of its own activity, which must be conceived as 'force' (*conatus*), 'energy' (*vis*), some 'tendency' (*appetitus*) or 'desire' (*cupiditas*) to realise what it is capable of (*quantum in se est*, as Spinoza is content to write) in time and space. This dynamic power Spinoza attributes to the 'essences' themselves, whereas Leibniz attributes it to 'monads' or 'metaphysical points'. In both cases, this leads to a radical nominalism (every individual is unique; 'there are exactly as many species as individuals', as Deleuze has it)[66] as well as to a definition of individuality which emphasises its complexity and, as a result, relativises the meaning of the opposition between 'wholes' and 'parts'. As we know, it is also this radical way of reorganising the logic of individuation that is often blamed for untenable or unacceptable theses concerning individual freedom. The difficulty obviously stems from the fact that, if one constructs the relations between individuals by incorporating them into other higher-level individualities, the autonomy of the parts seems to be absorbed entirely in the interest or the law of preservation of the whole, which seems difficult to allow when these 'parts' are precisely human beings.[67]

This is what Leibniz objects to in Spinozism, despite sharing its naturalism or 'immanentism'. Unlike Spinoza, Leibniz does not reject the theological concept of the original freedom of man: rather, he follows the path of Christian 'liberalism' that seeks to demonstrate that this freedom is fully compatible with divine providence and benevolence, in spite of original sin. This is the whole purpose of his *Essais de Théodicée*, his last major published work (1710), which in many ways is nothing but a refutation of Spinoza. It seems to me that this opposition is better understood if we reserve the term 'transindividuality' for Spinoza and that of 'intersubjectivity' for Leibniz. Husserl invented the latter term by referring directly to him.[68] It is not in Leibniz a question of actions and passions, but first of all of establishing correspondences between the representative contents of all the monads, which means that each one of them has a 'perception of the world' involving a clear or confused image of all the others. It could thus be said that, in Leibniz, all individual perceptions are nothing but different 'points of view' within the same horizon, and even that 'the world' is nothing else, in its essence, than the sum total of every individual's perceptions of all other individuals. As we know, this is what allows him to speak of a 'pre-established harmony' in which subjectivity and intersubjectivity are fully compatible with the idea of providence and the predetermination of the events of the world. But why does Leibniz think that he has thus preserved the freedom of human subjects? Precisely because freedom is thought of as a 'perfection', and a 'perfect' world (or at least, in our case, the 'most perfect of possible worlds') must include the greatest number of perfections compatible with its unity. The Leibnizian world includes in itself all conceivable degrees of freedom, from the lowest to the highest, according to a continuous progression. This means that there would be no human freedom in the chain of beings if there were not also an infinite quantity of comparatively 'less' free or, conversely, 'more' free beings. This does not imply, moreover, that all men are *equally free*, or enjoy 'equal freedom', because, although the analogy of form between humans also normally suggests an analogy between their liberties, the 'principle of indiscernibles' strictly prohibits the existence of two *equally free* men, and the 'principle of the best' suggests that this relative inequality is necessary for the constitution of the 'best of all possible worlds'. The conception of immanence that we are dealing with in Leibniz is therefore also profoundly hierarchical or, if you will, 'vertical'.

But is this the only way to understand the reciprocal determination of parts and the whole? One can also try to understand it in terms of a mutual implication between elementary 'individual' freedom and 'collective' freedom (or a freedom the conditions of which are collective).[69] Spinoza has made a particularly determined effort in this regard. His supposedly 'deterministic' – but in fact *causal* – doctrine seeks to define nature (of which society is a part) as a universal 'order-of-connection' of individualities. Is this incompatible with any notion of freedom, and therefore profoundly 'anti-humanist'? Spinoza responds, as we know, that it does not exclude real liberation – on the contrary, it must allow for the determination of its conditions – but rather only imaginary representations of freedom. When Spinoza declares desire (*cupiditas*) 'the very essence of man', and thus equates it with *vertu*, his intention is obviously not to propound a pessimistic anthropology, denouncing the natural selfishness of men and opposing this with an ideal of altruistic morality. His goal is to show that the affectivity that makes the human psyche 'oscillate' (*fluctuatio animi*) and the at once real and imaginary business of the transindividual are originally linked. It is to define a process of 'becoming necessary' of freedom itself which brings these two together from start to finish. 'Libertas . . . agendi necessitatem non tollit, sed ponit.'[70] The 'law' of this process is that the liberation of the individual actually multiplies collective power, just as collective freedom multiplies the power of the individual.

We are thus brought back to the divergence of the two systems. Initially, the divergence in their ways of understanding the immanence of difference to individuality appears minimal, but it remains irreducible and finally becomes a chasm, as metaphysical as it is political. It is obviously not a coincidence that Spinoza's philosophy aims at the construction of a democracy in which freedom of expression plays a constitutive role, and where, more generally, the diversity of individual opinions and free communication between individuals form a necessary condition for the existence of the state.[71] No doubt, there can be no pre-established harmony between the increasing power of individuals and that of the community. Their convergence can only be the result of a fragile equilibrium subject to fortune (that is, the effect of causes that rarely act together, and are easily held in check). This does prevent us from considering them as opposites. That is why I think we must, among the commentators, follow Matheron and with him those for whom, in the very moment when Spinoza gets closest to defining society as a 'market', is nevertheless at the antipodes of what will become 'liberalism', with its own metaphysics. On condition of establishing certain rules, individual 'powers' are virtually complementary to each other, but this complementarity is not automatic and must be constructed in their own activity.

Again, the confrontation with the Leibnizian conception of the individual illuminates crucial problems of Spinozism here. The *Monadology* as well as the *Essais de Théodicée* are indeed permeated by neo-Platonism, and their objective is overtly to provide a philosophical foundation for the Christian conception of personal identity, one which would not only be compatible with the dogmas of the immortality of the soul and the Last Judgement, but rationally intelligible. This is why every individual must have a singular relationship with God, thanks to which he will eventually be incorporated into the spiritual unity of humanity reconciled in the person of Christ (*corpus mysticum*).[72] To this mystical idea, Spinoza opposes a doctrine of *beatitudo* and *aeternitas*, which offers obvious difficulties, and even obscurities, but which undoubtedly tends to dissociate the capacity of the singular individual to attain the personal autonomy from Judeo-Christian beliefs which depict this autonomy as a 'salvation' achievable only in the beyond, outside the space and time of this world of misery. The doctrine outlined in this regard in Part V of the *Ethics* is as strange as it is remarkable, in that it posits that 'eternity' may be *partial* (or, relative to certain conditions, proportional): 'Qui Corpus ad plurima aptum habet, is Mentem habet, cujus maxima pars est aeterna'.[73] It is also remarkable in that it refers the Third Kind of Knowledge (and the corresponding *Amor intellectualis Dei*) to a form of 'consciousness' which is at the same time the specific causal knowledge of the one's own body and its affections qua powers. Finally, it is remarkable in that it describes the 'form' of this knowledge as an 'intellectual order' of ideas that would be exactly identical in the human understanding and in the divine understanding. That is why it can be thought *identically* in every human understanding, being perfectly indistinguishable there (but this can also be understood in an inverse sense: to say that the *ordinatio ad intellectum* of ideas is identical in the divine intellect and in human intellects is to take note of the fact that, through the difference of these, it remains identical to itself). Metaphysically speaking, there is no doubt that we are, here again, in the presence of an astonishing *coincidentia oppositorum*.

The interpretation I am proposing, based on the discussions above, is as follows. At the level of the Third Kind and intellectual eternity, there is no longer, apparently, any reference to the transindividual. But this does not in fact imply the reciprocal move: Spinoza explains to us what constitutes the highest (or supreme) degree of individuality, which an individual whose entire constitution is transindividual attains. To say that eternity is 'partial', or that it gives itself 'by parts', is to reject the idea of the *corpus mysticum* as an imaginary transposition of an inadequate idea that we have of our body onto the level of the 'whole' or the register of cosmic ideas. It is the counterpart of 'habemus enim ideam veram' of the *Tractatus de Intellectus Emendatione* (§27). Just as we are already in possession of some true (and therefore adequate) idea, so too can we already have the experience of the *beatitudo*. Eternity, therefore, has nothing to do with either a resurrection, a heaven, or even a promised land. It is that quality of our present existence which is active, or in which we ourselves are actively the cause of our preservation. 'Sentimus experimurque, nos aeternos esse.'[74]

As long as we are 'eternal' in this sense, our power to act and exist, and our power to think and understand is one and the same. Small wonder, then, that this activity goes along with our capacity to conceive of the multiplicity of our own body, as an effect of the many natural causes which it produces (and which are, from *our* point of view, 'pre-individual') as well as the way in which we consciously form ideas that transgress a 'restricted' or 'limitative' concept of the individual. Such ideas cannot be 'appropriated' *privately*, since they have exactly the same content in every mind, that is, in every part of the natural (infinite) power of thinking. These two complementary aspects of the doctrine expounded by Spinoza in Part V of the *Ethics* clearly refer to each of the 'attributes' of substance, so it seems that all the coherence of Spinoza's argument rests on the possibility – asserted from the outset – of thinking them as 'identical'. Which certainly contradicts common sense. But is this not because common sense is incapable of imagining that autonomy and community are not opposites, whose realisation would be inversely proportional? This allows us to return to finish off our initial hypothesis: what Spinoza is seeking to express in these paradoxical terms is an idea of the relationship between 'individuation' and 'individualisation' which would make the latter the very pre-condition of the former, and not the reverse, contrary to common sense as well as to the metaphysical tradition. This is why the transindividual in its active as well as passive modalities, expressing itself by the power of the imagination as much as by that of reason, remains the presupposition of this form of superior individuality that we have 'already' (more or less), but which also confers on it a higher power or quality in return.

## Notes

1 The same reasoning indeed applies to other propositions of the *Ethics* where some notion is identified as *ipsa hominis essentia*, notably Part IV, Definition 8, and the Demonstration of Proposition 20: 'Per virtutem et potentiam idem intelligo; hoc est . . . virtus, quatenus ad hominem refertur, est ipsa hominis essentia seu natura, quatenus' (By virtue and power I understand the same thing, i.e. . . . virtue, insofar as it is related to man, is the very essence, *or* nature, of man). Ontologically, they must be considered identical. This means that the 'real definition' cannot be enclosed in a single verbal formula. It is the *open* series of such equivalent propositions. But, since Spinoza is no formalist, they cannot be used indifferently in a given context. Their successive introduction is the underlying thread to the structure of the *Ethics*.
2 An implicit reference to the biblical question 'what is man?' is already present in the Appendix to Part I of the *Ethics*, where Spinoza rejects the picture of the world having been created by God for man's sake and benefit. Not by chance, this superstitious view of the 'place of Man in Nature' was identified with Man's consciousness of his appetites cum ignorance of the causes which determine them. The same critical position would result from the Preface to Part IV, where Spinoza discusses the ethical question of a 'model' (*exemplar*) of human nature.
3 More details on this point in É. Balibar, 'A Note on "Consciousness/Conscience" in the *Ethics*', *Studia Spinozana* 8 (1992), pp. 37–53. The first

English writer to have used 'consciousness' seems to be the Cambridge Platonist Ralph Cudworth, in his treatise directed against Hobbes and the 'materialists', *The True Intellectual System of the Universe*, published in 1678. But of course the meaning that became standard in modern philosophy was that proposed by Locke, in his *Essay on Human Understanding* (1690), especially after it had been translated into French by Pierre Coste (1700). See Catherine Glyn Davies, *Conscience as Consciousness: The Idea of Self-Awareness in French Philosophical Writing from Descartes to Diderot* (Oxford: Voltaire Foundation, 1990).

4  Such an opposition is indeed best known in modern social science as the *Gemeinschaft* versus *Gesellschaft* opposition, which was coined by Tönnies. But it has other formulations, developed over a long period. The word 'intersubjectivity' was introduced by E. Husserl (*Cartesianische Meditationen*: 1929; *Cartesian Meditations* [The Hague: Martinus Nijhof, 1950]) with direct reference to Leibniz and his 'monadology'. It clearly expresses the primacy of *interiority* (our relationship to a 'common', 'really existing' world of objects is mediated by the originary relationship of recognition between the *ego* and the *alter ego*). Quite differently, a moral and juridical tradition which can be traced back to Locke and Kant has opposed the moral community, which remains an ideal, located within each person's conscience, to the real civil society, which relies upon *exterior* institutions and obligations set up by law.

5  A. Matheron, *Individu et communauté chez Spinoza* (Paris: Éditions de Minuit, 1969).

6  Ibid., p. 164.

7  Ibid., p. 266.

8  Ibid., p. 275.

9  In his now famous book, *L'anomalia selvaggia* (*The Savage Anomaly*), Antonio Negri emphasises in particular the indisputable fact that the *Ethics* contains no use of the term 'substance' after the beginning of Part II (Proposition 10: 'substantia formam hominis non constituit'). The emphasis is from then on put on 'modes' and their infinite multiplicity (which includes the human mode). Everything happens as if the modes were emancipated from substance. Spinoza's ontology, as well as his politics, would henceforth be centred on nature as *multitudo*, as multiplicity and multitude, and not on unity. It seems to me, however, that if one understands substance in its properly Spinozist definition, that is to say, as universal causality, the two points of view of substance and modes are perfectly reciprocal. It is this reciprocity that is precisely at the heart of the problem of individuality.

10 On this point I part company with Matheron and align myself with Gueroult's position, as recently amended by P. Cristofolini, 'The dell'atomo mente', *Studia Spinozana* 8 (1992), pp. 27–35.

11 The fact that these two aspects are always present simultaneously – albeit to varying degrees – in the production of modes is the signature of Spinoza's 'naturalism', or if you like his anti-humanism: individuality as such is not a human characteristic, or, if you like, humans are not the only 'authentic' individuals. This necessarily results in the multiplicity of types of individuality, and at the limit their infinity (with 'similarities', which play a fundamental role in Spinozist ethics). Each individual is his own type (radical nominalism), and individuals are all the more useful to each other the more they are similar or, to use a better term, 'agree'.

12 This is, without doubt, one of the most profound meeting points between Spinoza and Leibniz, for both of whom individuation as individualisation is correlative to the interdependence of all individuals, in the figure of a network or system. Each in his own way, Spinoza and Leibniz realised that it is impossible in a strict sense to think of degrees of autonomy as associated with a 'strong' notion of singularity, without simultaneously positing a 'strong' – which is to say originary – notion of interaction and reciprocity of individuals. We may conclude that, in these philosophies, the object of true thought is not so much situated *at the extremes*, as in the classical opposition of the Whole and the Part (or the elementary), but concerns the reciprocity and the relativity of the 'points of view' expressed by the notions of the 'whole' and the 'part'. See Y. Belaval, 'Sur le simple et le composé', in *Études leibniziennes* (Paris: Gallimard, 1976). I will return to this comparison in my conclusion.

13 Gilbert Simondon, *L'individuation psychique et collective à la lumière des notions de Forme, Information, Potentiel et Métastabilité* (Paris: Aubier, 1989). This is the second half of Simondon's thesis (defended in the late 1950s), the first half of which appeared during his lifetime under the title *L'individu et sa genèse physico-biologique* (Paris: Presses universitaires de France, 1964). On Simondon's thought, see in particular Gilles Châtelet (ed.), *Gilbert Simondon. Une pensée de l'individuation et de la technique* (Paris: Albin Michel, 1994). Simondon's work is an ambitious and original attempt to redefine the ontological foundations of human sciences by criticising the concepts of individuality that proceed from Plato (individuality as finding its model outside itself, in archetypes that constitute invariant forms) or Aristotle (whose 'hylemorphic' schema aims to express the inner perfection of the individual), and which are always at work in the concepts of

natural philosophy or contemporary psychology (thus in *Gestalt* theorists). Simondon shows that the metaphysics of the individual based on classical antitheses (interior and exterior, *a priori* and *a posteriori*, psychologism and sociologism, etc.) always subordinate the intelligence of individuation or ontogeny to the definition of individuality as an ideally stable form. But contemporary physics and biology (in particular the study of the growth of crystalline structures and the biology of learning processes, where it is adaptation to a changing environment that requires the emergence of new structures) give us the means to think ontogeny differently. Stable forms that reduce potential energy to a minimum are less important in nature than *metastable* equilibria, which rely on maintaining a higher level of potential energy in the form of an individual-medium polarity. In this sense, Simondon's natural philosophy is a remarkable case of surpassing the antithesis between vitalism and reductionism, proceeding in ways different to Prigogine and Stengers' 'new alliance', which it antedates.

14 Negri also, of course, in *The Savage Anomaly* and in the more recent studies that extend this book, makes Spinozist ontology an analysis of the movement 'from the individual to the collective' without any 'imposition of continuity' (Negri, *The Savage Anomaly*, p. 136), a display of the power of the *multitudo* which organises itself, but it is at the price of the sacrifice of the whole theory of substance, and consequently of causality.

15 The view that I want to illustrate here implies also, at least for the central parts of the *Ethics*, the possibility, if not of breaking the unity of the 'parts' made autonomous by Spinoza (but transgressing the chain of derivation of propositions according to *the geometrical order*), at least of relativising its meaning (or, better still, emphasising the *transitions* that are the other side).

16 'Every singular thing, or any thing which is finite and has a determinate existence, can neither exist nor be determined to produce an effect unless it is determined to exist and produce an effect by another cause, which is also finite and has a determinate existence; and again, this cause also can neither exist nor be determined to produce an effect unless it is determined to exist and produce an effect by another, which is also finite and has a determinate existence, and so on, to infinity'

17 And more ultimately *vis-à-vis* the Aristotelian schema, to which Kant remains faithful. Proposition I, 28 of the *Ethics* can be understood only by contrast with Aristotle's formulations, opposing a 'circular demonstration' (which, at best, is reduced to a tautology) to linear or 'successive demonstration', especially in the *Posterior Analytics* (I, 3). By abandoning the linearity of the 'chain of causes', Spinoza can escape criticism of an

'infinite regress' (of which he will himself make polemical use, in the Appendix to Part I, against the finalist imagination's fascination with the question 'why').

18 'Nothing exists, from whose nature some effect does not follow. DEMONSTRATION: Whatever exists expresses the nature, *or* essence of God in a certain and determinate way, ... that is, ... whatever exists expresses in a certain and determinate way the power of God, which is the cause of all things. So ... some effect must follow' (Curley translation). Note the logical force of the double negation: *nothing* exists *that does not* necessarily produce effects, or, to put it another way, that is not also by that same token a *cause*.

19 On Spinoza's use of the terms *agere* and *operare*, see Pierre Macherey, 'Action et opération: sur la signification éthique du *De Deo*', in *Avec Spinoza. Etudes sur la doctrine et l'histoire du spinozisme* (Paris: Presses universitaires de France, 1992), p. 69 s.v. However, I part company with Macherey regarding the interpretation of Proposition 28, in which he sees a figure of 'bad infinity'.

20 'Mens res omnes necessarias esse intelligit, et infinito causarum nexu determinari ad existendum et operandum', as the proof of Proposition 6 of Part V will say, referring specifically to Propositions 28 and 29 of Part I ('The mind understands all things to be necessary, ... and to be determined by an infinite connection of causes to exist and produce effects. ... And so ... to that extent [the mind] brings it about that it is less acted on by the affects springing from these things, and ... is less affected toward them').

21 This is perfectly consistent with the negation of randomness, at least as it is classically defined, namely as a 'meeting of independent causal series'. Indeed, there are no 'independent series'. It is also clear what Spinoza's own reasons were for rejecting the notion of emptiness as incompatible with the idea of necessary connection in this sense (Scholium of Proposition 15 of Part I). Several commentators have sought to find models for this conception in older or more recent theories from physics (Gueroult and Parrochia with the theory of oscillations developed by Huygens, Bennett with field theory: all these have in common that they go from corpuscular intuitions to wave intuitions). Once again, Simondon's technical analogy, elaborated without reference to Spinoza, seems to me to be the best one: 'The term modulation ... designates the operation being carried out in an amplifying relay with an infinite number of states, like, for example, a hot cathode tube ... or a transistor. This is the operation by which a low energy signal, such as the one sent to the control gate of a triode, realises

with a certain number of possible degrees the potential energy represented by the anode circuit and the effector which is the external load of this circuit'. Simondon, *L'individuation psychique*, pp. 36–7.
22 *Ethics* Part I, Proposition 25, C, 'Particular things are nothing but affections of God's attributes, or modes by which God's attributes are expressed in a certain and determinate way'.
23 *Ethics* Part III, Definition 1 of the Affects.
24 See Chapter 1.
25 No one has better explicated the unity of the Kantian schema of causality and freedom ('causality out of freedom') than Heidegger in his course *On the Essence of Human Freedom: An Introduction to Philosophy*, trans. Ted Sadler (London: Continuum, 2002). 'Freedom is nothing other than *absolute natural causality*, or as Kant himself fittingly says, it is a concept of nature that transcends all possible experience' (p. 148).
26 'A thing is free, according to the law of its own action, or constraint, following the external chain of operations in which it is taken, according to whether it is considered from a global point of view or a partial point of view. To liberate oneself is therefore not to escape from the system of determination that necessarily links causes and effects, but on the contrary to enter into this system even more deeply, in order to grasp it, and thereby to assimilate its immanent necessity'. Macherey, 'Action et opération', p. 101.
27 There is therefore no need to distinguish, as Gueroult does, between exteriority and interiority, between existence as determined by the 'pressure of the environment' and existence as determined by the *conatus* of the essence: this would even be the misinterpretation to avoid, if one does not want to reintroduce in the long term a dualism of mechanical causes and final causes (as one finds for example in Leibniz).
28 Letter from Spinoza to Oldenburg, 20 November 1665: 'all bodies are surrounded by others, and are determined by one another to existing and producing an effect in a fixed and determinate ratio' (*sic*).
29 Ibid.: 'an effect in a fixed and determinate way, the same ratio of motion to rest always being preserved in all of them at once, that is, in the whole universe'. Spinoza, we know, distinguishes this formulation from Descartes's 'laws of nature'. But by replacing the Cartesian notion of a constant sum ('God . . . created matter with both movement and rest; and now maintains in the sum total of matter, by His normal participation, the same quantity of motion and rest as He placed in it' – *Descartes' Principles of Philosophy*, trans. V. R. Miller and R. P. Miller, Dordrecht: Kluwer, 1982,

p. 58) with that of constant ratio, he gives himself the means to make the levels of integration autonomous and to confer a relative dynamic stability upon individuals, who only have an apparent existence in the Cartesian 'extended substance', despite some 'whirlpools'. Cartesian laws themselves contrast with Aristotle's 'principles of movement', which concern the difference between 'natural' and 'artificial' beings: 'each has in itself a source of change and staying unchanged, whether in respect of place, or growth and decay, or alteration' (*Physics*, 192 b). The allusion remains recognisable in Spinoza, notwithstanding the transformation of the definitions of 'movement' and 'rest', and the substitution of the idea of ratio for that of principle (*arche*). This point is important because Aristotle then proceeds to explain the 'principle' as a 'natural [or intrinsic] tendency to change' (*hormè metabolès emphutos*), while Spinoza defines the *conatus* of individual essence as 'self-preservation'. Once again, Spinoza's physics, like his ontology, is extricated from the Aristotelian–Cartesian dilemma.

30 Let us be clear that, by these formulations, I do not mean to subscribe to the position defended, each in his own way, by Gueroult and by Bennett in Chapters 4 and 5 of *A Study of Spinoza's Ethics*, according to which Spinoza would have adopted two different doctrines or theories at different moments of his work, one a 'physics', the other a 'metaphysics'. On the contrary, Spinoza's 'physics' expresses exactly his ontology or conception of substance, according to the laws of extended attributes.

31 This is not a mere illusion, but the nature of the mind (*mens*) qua idea of the body, of which it reflects the actual existence. On this point, see *Ethics* Part II, Proposition 19.

32 'Those things are good which bring about the preservation of the ratio of motion and rest the human body's parts have to one another; on the other hand, those things are evil which bring it about that the parts of the human body have a different ratio of motion and rest to one another.'

33 It will be objected that this description takes into account only one of the three processes invoked by Spinoza in his explanation of the preservation of an individual form. The other two are: (1) change of the motion of one of its parts, under the effect of an external cause, provided that it is compensated for by an equivalent change in another part; and (2) change in size of the constituent parts of the individual who maintains the same *motus et quietis ratio*. Spinoza probably has different physiological phenomena in mind here. However, I believe that he is dealing with fundamentally the same process or the 'operation' of nature, albeit expressed in different language or by means of different images. The idea of a 'flow of input

and output' allowing a continual regeneration of the individual is of Epicurean origin, and corresponds to a discourse of particles. The core of the question is that Spinoza developed an idea of causality that goes beyond or integrates the perspectives of particles and of waves, each on its own constituting only a partial and therefore inadequate image of reality. Of course, 'constituent parts' can be imagined as pieces of matter as well as partial movements or components of movements, which are equally material, just as motion can be 'exchanged' or 'shared' just as well as parts. It is on this basis, it seems to me, that the question of the 'metaphorical' or 'conceptual' character of the whole explanation must rest.

34  It is from this scholium that François Zourabichvili has now reconstructed his own interpretation of all Spinoza's thought, from the ontology to the politics, as a theory of *mutatio formae*, leading to a 'paradoxical conservatism': F. Zourabichvili, *Le Conservatisme paradoxal de Spinoza. Enfance et royauté* (Paris: Presses universitaires de France, 2002).

35  To tell the truth, this case is privileged because the reader and the author of the *Ethics*, insofar as they are themselves men, or like men, have a particular interest in it, which makes it all the more important to free oneself from the imaginary, and to deal with it using 'common notions'.

36  During the oral presentation I made of these hypotheses in Rijnsburg, I generally spoke of 'decomposition', omitting to specify that it was 'virtual'. Professor Michiel Keyzer asked me what would happen if people did not accept being decomposed. This question, of course, seems crucial to me, not only because it highlights the immediate ethical (and political) significance of these 'physical' proposals, but because it raises the fundamental difficulty of knowing what is meant by 'actual' and 'virtual' in Spinoza. It seems to me that virtuality is indeed a Spinozist notion, which must not be confused with fiction or with possibility. Everything depends of course on the *point of view* one adopts, but points of view are themselves objective or real (which Spinoza expresses by saying that their idea exists in God). 'Parts of the human body' must therefore be considered both to belong to its essence ('quatenus motus suos certa quadam ratione invicem communicant') and, from a different point of view, to relate individually or separately to other external objects ('quatenus ut Individua, absque relatione ad humanum Corpus'). What I would suggest here is that the corresponding complete reality is an unstable equilibrium between two modes of existence, which correspond tendentially to activity and passivity. The question, then, is how such a balance evolves. This is what is at stake ethically: it is not in the power of natural individuals to become

indestructible, to form in units whose composition would be invariable. But it is in their power (that is to say, it belongs to their essence) to seek the conditions that will best preserve and strengthen the cohesion of their parts. What individuals 'want' is *not to be decomposed*; what they 'manage' to do at their own level, in the best case, is to *delay* (or perhaps modulate) *the actualisation of a virtual decomposition.*

37 What, in the case of political individuals or states, Spinoza calls the 'return to the mass' (*Political Treatise* 7.25, 8.3). I discussed this formulation ('ad multitudinem redire') in my article 'Spinoza, l'anti-Orwell: la crainte des masses', *Les Temps Modernes* 470, September 1985, now reissued in É. Balibar, *La crainte des masses. Politique et philosophie avant et après Marx* (Paris: Editions Galilée, 1997), in trying to show that Spinoza's 'statistics' involves a permanent process of decomposition and recomposition of the *multitudo*, as dangerous for governments as for the multitude itself.

38 'There is no singular thing in Nature than which there is not another more powerful and stronger. Whatever one is given, there is another more powerful by which the first can be destroyed' (Curley translation, quoted already in Chapter 1).

39 See in this regard Propositions 38 and 39 of Part V, and their Scholia.

40 In the vocabulary of affections, they increase joy and eliminate sadness for each individual.

41 In a rather unexpected way, the validity of the lone Axiom of Part IV seems to be limited by the Scholium of Proposition 37 of Part V: 'Partis Quartae Axioma res singulares respicit, quatenus cum relatione ad certum tempus et locum considerantur; de quo neminem dubitare credo' (Axiom of Part IV concerns singular things insofar as they are considered in relation to a certain time and place. I believe no one doubts this). This passage already explains, it seems to me, how we can hold that the point of view of the 'transindividual' is still at work in Part V, which is to say in the theory of the *amor intellectualis Dei* and the Third Kind of Knowledge. I will admit that this is not obvious unless we take Spinoza's 'political' texts together with the *Ethics* (following a suggestion made by Matheron, Negri and others), and ask that Spinoza's term 'aeternitas' and its correlates have an unambiguous meaning. The *Political Treatise*, in particular, explains that bodies politic, where the diversity of opinions reigns and is institutionally represented, are virtually 'eternal' (*Political Treatise* 8.3: 'concilia contra aeterna').

42 The comparison with Simondon's analyses becomes particularly illuminating here. The idea of a metastable equilibrium is that any individuation

remains dependent on a pre-individual potential from which the individual has emerged during successive 'structurations', of which there are as many as there are 'distanciations from the environment'. The very existence of individuals therefore always remains 'problematic' or 'tense'. It is this tension that individuals seek to resolve – or to understand – by acquiring, through building collectivities, a higher degree of individualisation. However, a living collectivity is neither a simple aggregate nor a fusion of pre-existing individuals: it must be a culture (what Simondon calls a 'spirituality', and which Spinoza would have described as a complex of reason and imagination), a dynamic solution to individual problems. This is why it must go back to the pre-individual level (especially the level of emotional patterns) to integrate them into a new metastable unity of a 'higher' order. This will thus be neither external nor internal to individuals, but precisely transindividual. 'It passes into the individual from the pre-individual, who is both a medium and an individual: it is starting from this, from this unresolved state, from this burden of reality that is still unindividuated, that man seeks his likeness to make up a group in which he will find a presence by a second individuation' (Simondon, *L'individuation psychique*, p. 192).

43 See on this theme P.-F. Moreau, *Spinoza. L'expérience et l'éternité* (Paris: Presses universitaires de France, 1994), especially pp. 379–465. The discussion I have just engaged in has been entirely in 'physical' terms, which is to say that it posits, in accordance with Spinoza, that individuals are first and foremost 'bodies' (and are individualised as bodies). But it is also necessary to ask how the same idea might be expressed in the attribute of thought (*cogitatio*), that is to say, insofar as individuals are minds (*mentes*). I would suggest, subject to discussion, that this correlate should be sought in the theory of the *idea ideae*, an expression which in the *Ethics* appears only in Part II, in close correlation with the definition of the composition of individuals and of the *mens* as *idea corporis*. In Parts III, IV and V, the *idea ideae* becomes implicit, at the same time as Spinoza takes up the point of view of the *mens* as a complex of ideas of the affections of the body, for which he describes the variable modes of connection and transformation. Let us remark here that, in the language of the 'mental', *convenientiae* are none other than *notiones communes*, provided that we understand them not only from the point of view of their universal 'objective' content, but also in their 'formal' being as collective modes of thought.

44 'It is impossible that a man should not be a part of Nature, and that he should be able to undergo no changes except those which can be

understood through his own nature alone, and of which he is the adequate cause' (Curley translation).

45  Proposition 1 of Part III ('Our Mind does certain things [acts] and undergoes other things, viz. insofar as it has adequate ideas, it necessarily does certain things, and insofar as it has inadequate ideas, it necessarily undergoes other things') involves a whole phenomenology of affective life and follows it by immediately 'translating' these principles into mental language, in accordance with the theses of Part II.

46  I draw many useful ideas here from Michèle Bertrand, *Spinoza et l'imaginaire* (Paris: Presses universitaires de France, 1983), who brings Freud's lessons to bear in reading Spinoza, while at the same time highlighting the inconsistencies between the two thinkers.

47  'This *constitution of the Mind, which arises from two contrary affects* is called *vacillation of mind*, which is therefore related to the affect as doubt is to the imagination. . . . But it should be noted that in the preceding Proposition I have deduced these vacillations of mind from causes which are the cause through themselves of one affect and the accidental cause of the other. I have done this because in this way they could more easily be deduced from what has gone before, not because I deny that vacillations of mind for the most part arise from an object which is the efficient cause of each affect. For the human Body . . . is composed of a great many individuals of different natures [ex plurimis diversae naturae individuis componitur], and so, . . . it can be affected in a great many different ways by one and the same body. And on the other hand, because one and the same thing can be affected in many ways, it will also be able to affect one and the same part of the body in many different ways. From this we can easily conceive that one and the same object can be the cause of many and contrary affects' (*Ethics* Part III, Proposition 17, Scholium).

48  'From the mere fact that we imagine a thing to have some likeness to an object that usually affects the Mind with Joy or Sadness, we love it or hate it, even though that in which the thing is like the object is not the efficient cause of these affects' (*Ethics* Part III, Proposition 16).

49  'If we imagine a thing like us, toward which we have had no affect, to be affected with some affect, we are thereby affected with a like affect' (*Ethics* Part III, Proposition 27).

50  It seems to be particularly important to Spinoza, from an ethical point of view, to limit this process of association, which is rooted in the *partial images* of the body and mind, *to other human (objects)*, despite how difficult it is to impose such a restriction. The two excesses or confusions

that concern him here are, on the one hand, identification with animals (zoophilia and zoophobia), and on the other anthropomorphising God as either benevolent or malicious ('jealous'). It may well be that this is a crucial aspect of what Spinoza goes on to discuss in Part V as the problem of the causal understanding of one's own body and its actual *potentia*.

51 See in particular the definitions of *ambitio* and *humanitas* in the Scholium of Proposition 29. It is precisely from this that the explanation of imaginary sociability, or, better, the explanation of sociability *as far as* it is the result of the imagination, proceeds. Propositions 43–6 explain 'class' and 'national' identities in particular in these terms. Proposals 32–4 and the second Scholium of Proposition 37 will explain the constitution of civil society by reference to the *fear of the differences* that each individual imagines as incompatible with their own preservation. I have discussed this myself in more detail in Étienne Balibar, *Spinoza and Politics*, trans. Peter Snowdon (New York: Verso, 1998), pp. 77ff.
52 *Ethics* Part IV, Proposition 18, Scholium.
53 In terms of the famous tripartition proposed by Lévi-Strauss at the end of *The Elementary Structures of Kinship*, one could say that (in the *Ethics* in any case) Spinoza is not concerned (in spite of Aphorisms 27–9 of Appendix of Part IV, on the food of the body and the use of money and thus on its 'fetishism' dominating the minds of the vulgar) with the exchange of goods, but, rather, with the exchange of women (or more precisely objects of sexual love) and the exchange of words (or more generally signs, even if it is only in the *Theological Political Treatise* that he attempts to analyse linguistic communication as such).
54 And also to oppose it to other well known formulas: neither *homo homini lupus* nor *homo homini deus* (two formulations which rather characterise the ambivalent representations of the imagination), but a 'tautology' (doubtless very difficult to observe in practice), *homo homini homo*, which is to say, *res utilis*, or even *utilisissima*. A 'plane of immanence', one might say, à la Deleuze.
55 'Only insofar as men live according to the guidance of reason, must they always agree in nature' (*Ethics* Part IV, Proposition 35).
56 'This Love toward God cannot be tainted by an affect of Envy or Jealousy: instead, the more men we imagine to be joined to God by the same bond of Love, the more it is encouraged' (*Ethics* Part V, Proposition 20).
57 *Ethics* Part IV, Proposition 66, Scholium.
58 I know of only one point in the *Ethics* where Spinoza explicitly notes this consequence implied by his theory of reason, by means of an example

which is both surprisingly symptomatic and surprisingly generic at the same time: the Scholium of Proposition 68 of Part IV, where he interprets the biblical story of Adam, opposing the rational community of Adam and Eve to imaginary similarities between humans and animals: 'This and the other things I have now demonstrated seem to have been indicated by Moses in that story of the first man . . . man having found a wife [inventa ab homine uxore] who agreed completely with his nature, he knew that there could be nothing in nature more useful to him than she was; but that after he believed the lower animals to be like himself, he immediately began to imitate their affects [postquam bruta sibi similia esse credidit, status eorum affectus imitari inceperit], and to lose his freedom'.

59 *Ethics* Part IV, first Scholium of Proposition 37, and Proposition 70.
60 Notably in Proposition 59 of Part IV – 'To every action to which we are determined from an affect which is a passion [ex affectu, qui passio est], we can be determined by reason, without that affect' – and its Scholium.
61 We have here, if we think about it, a truly astonishing transformation of the formula by which Aristotle defined *politeia* (the constitution of citizenship) in the Book III of the *Politics*: every citizen (excluding other men) is sometimes active and sometimes passive under 'command' (*arche*): *archôn* and *archomenos*.
62 *Ethics* Part IV, Proposition 18, Scholium.
63 The question *quod sit homo*, to which Spinoza dedicates himself from the beginning of Part III of the *Ethics*, offering several formulations whose equivalence is problematic, has two literary sources, one in the Bible ('quid est homo, quod memor es ejus?' Psalm 8 asks God) and the other in Greek philosophy (Plato, *Alcibiades*, Aristotle, etc.). Some of the ideas I present here are already in my essay 'What is "man" in 17th century philosophy? Subject, individual, citizen', in J. Coleman (ed.), *The Individual in Political Theory and in Practice* (Oxford: Oxford University Press, 1996), pp. 215–41.
64 Matheron rightly insists on this point in his essay 'L'anthropologie spinoziste', in *Anthropologie et politique au XVIIe siècle: Etudes sur Spinoza* (Paris: Vrin 1986), pp. 17–27.
65 This is a unifying factor of his two books, *Expressionism in Philosophy: Spinoza* (New York: Zone, 1990) and *The Fold: Leibniz and the Baroque* (Minneapolis: University of Minnesota Press, 1993).
66 See in particular *Expressionism in Philosophy*, pp. 197–9.
67 As I noted above, there is something in Spinoza's doctrine that immediately disturbs this type of reading: the fact that the integration of individuals into higher individualities, which their own preservation depends, can only

be accomplished on condition of a decomposition (which I have called 'virtual') of their own individuality. Now, this decomposition is never unequivocal; it can be accomplished according to a very large number of different modalities which have no equivalence between them. The *determination* of the best modalities of decomposition–recomposition, or of the constitution of the reciprocal belonging of individuals, is, for Spinoza, both the stakes and the content of ethical liberation.

68 Husserl introduces the term 'intersubjectivity' in a series of manuscripts leading to his 1929 *Cartesianische Meditationen*. Those manuscripts are now available in French: E. Husserl, *Sur l'intersubjectivité*, translation, Introduction, Postface and index by Natalie Depraz (Paris: Presses universitaires de France, 2001, 2 vols). The concept of intersubjectivity implies that our relationship to a 'common' world in which we situate the reality of objects is mediated by an originary recognition of the *ego* and *alter ego*: it therefore emphasises *interiority*, as does the Leibnizian monad (which, according to the well known formula that Kant denounces as amphibology, 'has no outside'). On the other hand, I will not say that the Spinozian conception of the transindividual belongs to a 'thought of the outside' in the strict sense, but, rather, that it constantly 'problematises' the very distinction between interior and outside.

69 Which is also to say, from the point of view of the history of political ideas, between the 'liberty of the moderns' and the 'liberty of the ancients', that 'after' and that 'before' liberalism, to quote Quentin Skinner, *Liberty Before Liberalism* (Cambridge: Cambridge University Press, 1998).

70 *Political Treatise* 2.11.

71 The *Tractatus Theologico-Politicus* says this expressly, but the *Tractaus Politicus* does not deny it. See my *Spinoza and Politics*.

72 On the unity of Leibniz's metaphysical and eschatological views, see the essay by Michel Fichant accompanying his edition of Leibniz's fragment, *De l'horizon de la doctrine humaine* (*Apokatastasis pantôn: La Restitution Universelle*) (Paris: Vrin, 1991), especially pp. 204ff. ('Progrès spirituel et individualité').

73 'He who has a Body capable of a great many things has a Mind whose greatest part is eternal' (*Ethics* Part V, Proposition 39).

74 *Ethics* Part V, Scholium to Proposition 23.

# 3

# *Potentia multitudinis, quae una veluti mente ducitur*

In the following discussion, I will pursue a simple aim, but one which seems to me to raise fundamental questions for Spinozism: to try to explain the strange phrase used by Spinoza, notably at the beginning of Section 2 of Chapter 3 of the *Political Treatise*, 'potentia multitudinis, quae una veluti mente ducitur'. This phrase (other occurrences of which I will canvass momentarily) comes at a key moment in the treatise's argument, after Spinoza has equated 'right' with 'power' and then posited a fundamental distinction between the two possible statuses for individuals (dependence and independence; *esse alterius juris* and *esse sui juris*). He at this point sets out to define the nature of the power of the state and its relation, on the one hand, with the classical concept of 'sovereignty', and on the other with the distribution of rights and duties among citizens. However, this phrase has never ceased to confuse interpreters, because of the restrictive modality indicated by the preposition *veluti*, which seems to connect dubiously to the reference to a *mens* (soul or mind) of political communities – and consequently also to their 'bodies' or 'corporeality' (*corpus*). Some interpreters pass over this very quickly; others, on the contrary, discuss it at length, invoking fundamental propositions of Spinoza's system. But all consider there to be a difficulty to clear up.

To try to determine what is at stake in this formulation, I will proceed by means of an expanding circle of considerations. I propose first to 'read', to the letter, Spinoza's phrase (referring to various translations as needed), to clarify what is (or may seem to be) paradoxical in it. I will then explore how different notable interpretations of Spinoza's formula stand in relation to one another, privileging those of Matheron, Rice and Negri, and then that of P.-F. Moreau, which is based on the critical examination of the preceding ones and tries to go beyond their aporias, but which I will nevertheless explain does not satisfy me fully. To overcome this difficulty, I will examine the Spinozist formulation in a series of contexts, so as to state the principles in which I think a solution must lie. Paradoxically, while my solution is meant to be 'literal' or 'literalist', it will entail shifting certain accepted ideas of Spinoza's system, which will bring me, in conclusion (although to be really rigorous, this would require a further presentation), to sketch a return to two even more general questions: that of the function of the concept of *mens*, and that of the relations between 'individuality', 'causality' and 'adequation' in Spinoza's doctrine – suggesting thereby that the stakes of this seemingly very particular problem could be the measure of his entire system.

## A Paradoxical Restriction?

Let me start by quoting Spinoza's sentence in its entirety, so that the syntactic articulations are clearly visible:

> 1. patet imperii, seu summarum potestatum Jus nihil esse praeter ipsum naturae Jus, quod potentia, non quidem uniuscujusque, sed multitudinis, quae una veluti mente ducitur, determinatur,

> hoc est, quod [sicuti] unusquisque in statu naturali, sic etiam totius imperii corpus¹ et mens tantum juris habet, quantum potentia valet.

It will be useful here to have arrayed a choice of translations in several languages, so as to show the variations of interpretation that they imply. I have selected four particularly authoritative ones: in English, that of Edwin Curley; in French, that of Pierre-François Moreau; in Italian, that of Paolo Cristofolini; in German, that of Wolfgang Bartuschat:

> 2. it's evident that the Right of a state, *or* of the supreme powers, is nothing more than the Right of nature, determined not by the power of each person, but by the power of a multitude, led as if by one mind. That is, just as person in the natural state has as much power, so the body and mind of the whole state have as much right as they have power.²

> 3. le droit de l'Etat, ou du pouvoir souverain n'est rien d'autre que le droit même de la nature. Il est déterminé par la puissance, non plus de chaque individu, mais de la multitude, qui est conduite comme par un seul esprit; autrement dit, comme c'est le cas à l'état naturel, pour chaque individu, le corps et l'esprit de l'Etat tout entier ont autant de droit que de puissance.³

> 4. il diritto dello stato, ossia del potere sovrano, non è altro se non il diritto stesso di natura, determinato dalla potenza non di un singolo, ma del popolo, come guidato da una sola mente; vale a dire che, come un singolo allo stato di natura, così pure il corpo e la mente dell'intero stato hanno tanto diritto quanta è la potenza che possono far valere.⁴

> 5. das Recht des Staats oder der höchsten Gewalten nichts anderes ist als eben das Recht der Natur, das durch die Macht,

nun nicht mehr jedes einzelnen, sondern der wie von einem
Geist geleiteten Menges bestimmt wird. Gerade so wie im Fall
eines einzelnen im Naturzustand also auch der Körper und der
Geist eines ganzen Staats so viel Recht, wie weit dessen Macht
reicht.[5]

Several problems seem to me to be posed by a strict reading of
this passage. The first is the question of what kind of relative
clause, 'defining' or 'non-defining', is introduced here by *quae*.
Should we understand that the right/power of the state or of
the sovereign, considered as a single individuality, is determined
by the power of the *multitudo*, *since* this is done 'as if by one
mind' (or a single soul), or *when* (*to the extent that*) it is done
'as if by one mind'? Moreau, as in Latin, balances between the
two possibilities. Bartuschat, without absolutely excluding the
'defining' solution (that it is the essence of the multitude to be
led as by one mind) nonetheless employs a phrasing that is more
suggestive of the 'non-defining' interpretation (that the *multitudo*
or *Menge* which determines the power of the state is not just any
'mass', but *this one that* acts as if by one mind). Cristofolini, on
the contrary, clearly veers towards the first sense, cohering in
this with his translation (not unreasonable in a political context)
of *multitudo* by *popoli*;[6] what he suggests, in short, is that the
people is a mass or multitude acting 'as if guided by one single
soul', and as such determines the power of the state, which is to
say that it is its base or substance. In the one case, one will be
left trying to decide under what conditions a multitude can be
unified by a direction that confers on it a single mind or soul. In
the other – starting from the principle *omnia sunt animata* – one
will be left trying to understand why Spinoza hesitates to name
the *mens* corresponding to this individualised 'body' that is a
people constituted in a state.

This first difficulty is redoubled by a second: what is the fairest way to evaluate the modality introduced by *veluti*? What term or group of terms can it sensibly refer to? Ultimately (given the plasticity offered by Latin syntax) three possibilities exist: *veluti* relates to the whole action (it is as if the multitude were guided by one mind or one soul); *veluti* is the agent (it is as if the multitude were guided by a single mind, in other words as if there were one mind guiding it); or *veluti* relates specifically to the *una* (which is perhaps stylistically the most satisfying solution: it is as if the mind or the soul – or even the thought, as Appuhn renders it in his translation, to which I will return – that guides the multitude in the state were unique or unified). The point of making this distinction is to take us from one extreme to the other apropos of the question of the *mens* in relation to the multitude, just as we did above with the question of the *multitudo* in relation to the *imperium*. It would seem, then, that the clause that begins *hoc est* ('that is to say'), taken as a whole, is meant to clear up our uncertainty, and on two points at the same time: 'hoc est, quod sicuti unquisuque in statu naturali, sic etiam totius imperii corpus, et mens tantum juris habet, quantum potentia valet'. But all this explication has done in reality is make us confused.

This explication is based on a comparison (*sicuti*) between the individuality of the singular man ('in the state of nature', which is to say also according to nature) and that of the *imperium* (which gives form, and thus body, to the *multitudo*). But either:

1. Spinoza introduced a restriction only to humour the reader, who is not ready to consider the state, or the body politic, as an individual in the full sense, with all the consequences which this entails for Spinozist theory, in particular the existence of a mind as the 'idea of the body' corresponding

exactly to that 'body'. Decisively, now, rigorously applying the same law of composition to all the individualities at different levels (or of different complexity, some of which are 'parts' of the others), he posits the correlative existence of a *corpus* and a *mens* in relation to all individualities, and notably does so *in the same sense* in relation to the human individual as in relation to the political individual (the *Civitas* which is both *imperium* and *multitudo*), implicitly generalising the Scholium of Proposition 7 of Part II of the *Ethics*. This rigorous thesis would remove all ambiguities and serve as a basis for the deductions that come afterwards concerning the nature of the state and its different forms (in particular all those concerning the *preservation of its own form*). But how is it, then, that the expression *una veluti mente duci* figures massively, in an almost hackneyed way, sometimes about *homines* and sometimes about the *multitudo* itself, *in the many passages of the* Political Treatise *where Spinoza also evokes the question of the unity and individuality of the 'body politic' and the 'mental reality' that corresponds to it* (to mention one of the equivalences proposed by Macherey), both *before* and *after* Chapter 3 of Part II? And how is it that he meanwhile invokes the *corpus*–*mens* dyad in an 'absolute' way only exceptionally in relation to the city or state?

Or, conversely:

2. The restrictive modality contained in the *veluti*, however it is construed within Spinoza's first proposition (as a reservation, an approximation, an analogy, or the mark of a hypothesis), continues to apply to the second proposition and the comparison that that proposition sets out. The possibility of

speaking in terms of the *corpus* and *mens* of a state – given that the state is never anything other than the gathering or the expression of the power of the multitude – ought always to take into account that the *mens* in question here only has a metaphorical identity (in the words of Lee C. Rice). What Spinoza meant to say, then, is that, no doubt, the constitution of a 'body politic' illustrates general theorems concerning individuation (which we could ironically express, taking up the famous formula of the Preface to Part III of the *Ethics*, by saying that the *imperium* or the political state is not in nature *veluti imperium in imperio*, not like 'a state within a state'), but that the comparison between several types of individuality founders immediately on an unavoidable dissymmetry. The *mens* would not be collective *in the true sense*, but only an *effect* of mental or psychic unity, manifested in a 'conduct' or 'direction' of the state mixed in practice with the exercise of sovereignty. But if that is so, confusing consequences seem to follow. In particular, once there is doubt about the reality of the collective unity or the set of ideas, designated here analogically by the term *mens*, which evokes the conception of the human mind propounded in the *Ethics* but which no longer corresponds exactly to it, *how can we prevent that doubt also affecting the possibility of characterising the city or the state as a body* in the strict sense of the term, which is to say as a material individual that tends to preserve itself by virtue of its own essence or law of composition?

Let us note the close relationship of this problem with the question of interpretation posed by other formulas, both in the *Political Treatise* and in the *Ethics*. This is the case especially for the formulation that Spinoza uses in the Scholium of Proposition 18 of Part IV of the *Ethics*, which is all the more interesting because it proposes an ideal genesis of collective individuality from the junction (or composition) of the forces of two or more simple individualities according to their natural 'convenience', or their reciprocal usefulness: 'nihil, inquam, homines praestantius ad suum esse conservandum, optare possunt, quam quod omnes in omnibus ita conveniant, ut omnium Mentes et Corpora unam quasi Mentem, unumque Corpus componant, et omnes simul, quantum possunt, suum esse conservare conentur'.[7] One could of course suppose that the *quasi* (which is extremely close to our *veluti*) relates here only to the unity of the soul, leaving intact that of the body. But not only would that reading be contrary to the norms of Latin rhetoric (which seeks a symmetry of meaning in the dissymmetry of construction),[8] it would render unintelligible the explanatory position that the formulation of the *Ethics* occupies with respect to the various formulations of the *Political Treatise*.

We should now indeed remind ourselves that, in this latter work, besides the many occurrences of the expression 'una veluti mente ducitur', we also find a symmetrical formula, relating to the body, which shifts the element of approximation or analogy: 'necesse ergo est, ut Patricii omnes legibus ita astringantur, ut unum veluti corpus, quod una regitur mente, componant'.[9] Here, it is the presumed unity of the soul which provides on the side of the body the analogue of an autonomous individuality. *Everything happens as if, in any case, the individuality perceived from one side (should we say 'under one of the attributes'?) always proves to be problematic or deficient from the other side (one might say 'under the other attribute')*, which the text of the *Ethics* would explain precisely by stating that, in the last analysis, the composition of the individual human *conatus* in a political collective only produces the *analogue* of a higher individuality, but never one in the true sense. The designation of the city as an 'individual', a term which Spinoza uses because of his desire to address all ethical, political and anthropological questions according to the principles of natural knowledge, and because of his need to explain the *transfer of rights* between the sovereign and the particular subject (citizen) that gives rise to the formation of a city, is therefore permanently affected by an internal vacillation.

But we are likely to face an even more confusing problem. Many of the formulas that I have just mentioned are in fact based on the analogy between the masses or institutions assimilated to the 'body' of the state on one side,[10] while *mens* (or sometimes *caput*: *Political Treatise* 9.14) refers to an instance of command, decision or legislation. This analogy is certainly classical (dating as far back as the fable of Menenius Agrippa at least), but one must agree that it contradicts the schema of intelligibility commonly referred to as parallelism, which it would be better to describe (after the description given in the Part II of *Ethics*) as the *identity of difference* between 'orders' and 'connections' of ideas (which together form the *mens*) and things (primarily those of the *corpora*).[11] It seems, then, that we are faced with an unhelpful choice of alternatives. On the one hand, the recognition of the individuality of bodies politic or states is at least *a contrario* in the spirit of 'parallelism', which is to say that individuality is produced *or not* along with a material cohesion of parts and an intellectual or more generally mental unity, so in the form of a thought that is collective or applies to the collective. But on the other hand the mechanism of unification, insofar as it must be described *politically*, as a game of forces or powers and of institutions, can only be presented as an effect of mental activity (deliberation, decision, and representation) on the congruence of the body, devoid of ontological significance if not completely absurd from a Spinozist point of view.

## Some problematic solutions

These difficulties have already seen wide discussion among readers of the *Political Treatise*. I will mention only four justly famous interpretations. I will call the first three 'dogmatic', not to denigrate them, but because they all imply – albeit in opposite directions – that the solution lies immediately in a correct understanding of Spinozism, which they propose to develop. Moreau's interpretation, however, can be called 'critical' since, coming after all the others, he considers their opposition itself to be part of the problem, and undertakes to construct a hypothetical solution that seeks in the texts the means of satisfying the questions that their confrontation poses.[12]

### *The dogmatic solutions*

*1. Matheron*
I would first like to reflect on some particularly interesting thoughts of Matheron, who has returned to this subject several times. In *Individu et communauté chez Spinoza*, he opens his reconstruction of Spinozist politics with an analysis of the relationships between the three questions of individuation, complexity (or the nature of relations between all parties) and adequation (therefore also of the inadequacy of both ideas and causes) entirely based on the propositions of the *Ethics*, in which he thus sees (as Spinoza himself indicated) the basis

of all intelligibility of the propositions relating to politics. He proposes to follow this path of explanation entirely rigorously. As a result, he references the *Political Treatise* only much later in the piece. On pages 346–7 of his original French, Matheron dwells on the formulation of the *Political Treatise* 4.1: 'Jus summarum potestarum, quod earum potentia determinatur . . . in hoc potissimum consistere vidimus, nempe quod imperii veluti mens sit, qua omnes duci debent'.[13] From there, he goes back to our proposition concerning the *potentia multitudinis*. He thus gets over a cleavage between the two terms that *Political Treatise* 3.2 identifies (by means of *seu*, a well known term in Spinoza) – the *imperium* and the *summa potestas* (the state and the sovereign) – and he makes the restriction expressed by *veluti* apply only to the second term, suggesting that the state (or the body politic) is indeed an 'individual', as such endowed with a 'mind', but that the sovereign represents only a part of it. The fundamental question (which is political as well as ontological) then becomes one of knowing under what conditions this 'mind' of the sovereign (that is to say, in Spinozist terms, this set of ideas which are those of the sovereign alone) can be brought to coincide with the mind of the state itself. We can guess that, as a general rule, this correspondence is meant to be only partial, or that it must remain inadequate, except perhaps, at the end of the evolution of political societies towards maximum rationality and power, in the case of the democratic *imperium*.

Not only does this reading violate the letter of the *Political Treatise* 3.2 (evading in particular the *hoc est . . . etiam totius imperii corpus et mens*),[14] but it also avoids facing up to the difficulty contained in Spinoza's *general* propositions concerning the power of the multitude and the 'sovereign' way in which it incorporates (or combines) the powers of the citizens in the framework of *any* state. On the other hand, it has the advantage of suggesting (and I will come back to this point) that Spinoza's definitions and inferences can be read not so much as descriptions of *existing forms* or characteristics of a *given essence* of the state, but, rather, as the index of a *process,* or of a *transition* always already in progress in the life of states, which would constitute the true object of political theory. This transition is oriented towards the full realisation of the democratic 'powers' inherent in any state, but obviously not guaranteed to result therein.

It is striking that Matheron's ideas have given rise to quite different articulations among his most faithful followers: I am thinking in particular of Laurent Bove (who purely and simply eliminates the cautiousness of Spinoza's language in favour of a 'teleological structure' in the history of the state, based on the democratic essence of the collective *conatus*)[15] and Christian Lazzeri (who sees in Spinoza's formulas individualising the people or the state, with their 'bodies' and their 'minds', a metaphor directed against Hobbes, to show that the multitude, 'the natural set of individuals', can be directed only by virtue of its own consent, where the convergence of everyone's desires is expressed).[16] The most interesting thing of all is probably the way Matheron, since then, has come to clarify and transform his position. Thus, in a later study,[17] he takes up the question *negatively*, starting from the indignation of the multitude (which Spinoza says constitutes the very *limit* of sovereignty), showing that it not only forms the basis of revolutions, but that of states themselves, insofar as states' power is organised precisely to thwart the passional mechanisms (the *imitation of affects*) according to which it operates. However, indignation, which is a form of interpersonal hatred, is 'necessarily bad'. There is, therefore, in the construction of the state a sort of double bind, which clarifies the modality of Spinoza's *una veluti mente ducitur*: grappling with the necessity of 'conformism' in the multitude at the same time as with its formidable dangers (Matheron goes so far as to say that, according to Spinoza, 'the basic form of democracy is lynching'), the state must at the same time be based on citizens' unanimity and depart from it constantly. The difficulty of maintaining such a position could also be 'one of the reasons for the incompleteness of the *Political Treatise*'. Apparently turning his back on ontological considerations about individuality, Matheron here embarks on a sociological, almost Tocquevillian path, by which he succeeds in perfectly representing how insistent the Spinoza of the *Political Treatise* is. But in doing so, he restricts himself to the problematic of consensus and the regulation of opinions, apparently leaving to one side the question of decisions, which in Spinoza's text are, however, inseparable from one another.

## 2. Rice

Rice begins by contrasting a completely opposite reading to what he perceives to be Matheron's 'organicism', one which places him, on the contrary, on the side of 'methodological individualism' (and at the same time undertakes to reclaim this method for a liberal politics, from the Hegelian and Marxist tradition's hold on it).[18] But the most interesting aspect of his study, to my mind, resides in the fact that, pushing the examination of the problems raised by such a reading to its limit, he is led to reformulate the question of the logic of the modalities inherent in 'naturalism'.

Rice considers the organicist interpretation (which he also calls 'literalist' because it means to take the expression 'individual' literally when applied to bodies politic) to be based on an erroneous interpretation of the development of the argument of the *Ethics* (Part II after Proposition 13) regarding simple and compound bodies as extending its naturalistic scope to the collectives whose social and cognitive functions are being analysed, whereas it actually concerns only living organisms. Politics is thus replaced by an ontology (summed up in the idea that the state as such possesses a *conatus*), and the intrinsic equivocation of the notion of individuation is ignored in favour of a general schema of integration of wholes of increasing complexity.[19] Such a reading – which may take various forms, physicalist or vitalist – is the source of 'holistic' uses of Spinoza's political thought that make him the precursor to Hegel and Marx.[20] By contrast, Rice sees him as a fundamentally nominalist philosopher who champions morality and a politics of radical individualism. His 'communal unities' essentially result from individuals' perception of their reciprocal utility, which leads them to flee solitude and to unite as a function of their circumstances.[21] Therefore, as argued by McShea and Den Uyl, the formation of collectives (which are always 'historical' or 'contingent') is not an individuation but a more or less complete harmonisation (which precisely indicates the modality of the *veluti una mente* here) based on the laws of psychology. This would imply two types of radically distinct causality, only the first of which relates to the formation of a *conatus*. This is because, as shown by the comparison between the schema of integration set out in Letter 32 and the political works, in one case the activity of the parties can be *deduced* from the law of the composition of everything, whereas this determination is absolutely excluded in the other (that is to say, in the case of political communities, and indeed Spinoza never argued that the citizenry themselves act with the function of or with a view to preserving the state of which they are parts). As a result, while it is characteristic of individual organisms to represent a power *higher* than that of the parts that compose it, such a representation is ruled out for political totalities, the power of which is *less* than the sum of the powers of their individual constituents. Hence Spinoza's insistence that they 'preserve' their 'natural Right' within society (Letter 50).

Having drawn this dividing line, Rice warns against misinterpretation: it is not a question of claiming that socio-political collectives are less 'real' than organic individuals, but of showing that, from Spinoza's point of view, they do not have the same epistemological status. Therefore Spinoza would never have defended the idea of a *science of politics*, not even in the same sense in which there can be a 'psychological science' that deduces laws of individual human behaviour from the nature of the passions. The study of socio-historical phenomena (for example the history of peoples or the greater or lesser stability of political regimes) is not, for him, science (in the strictest sense of something that deals with the idea of nature and natural laws), but only empirical observation and generalisation.

This argument leads to a very interesting alternative to the thesis that sees in the formation of 'political individuals' the *level of integration immediately above* the formation of human organisms: if this level is not that of society, it must be imagined as one of supra-individual natural integration, intermediate between the laws of the composition of organisms and those of the *facies totius universi* that Spinoza posits as the 'ultimate' individuality. Contemporary developments in physics and biology suggest hypothetically (but not implausibly) the possibility here of inserting a notion like that of the *ecosystem*, which is to say of an integrated natural environment having its own laws of equilibrium. And then it becomes very tempting to develop 'Spinozist epistemology' in the way that Goodman's semantics today suggest, by which even the notion of the individual is relative to a theoretical framework, and the fundamental epistemological problem is that of the modality of the laws necessary within a given theory when we include them in a theory of higher order.[22] Even if it is doubtful, Rice says, that Spinoza was inclined to adopt the thesis of a 'contingency of the necessity' of laws of nature superimposed on the systems which they concern, the evidence does not show such a thesis to contradict his principles.

As interesting as it may be, this thesis nevertheless seems to me to have two difficulties, by its own lights. The first is that Rice vacillates between two uses of the term 'metaphor': sometimes he means by this the metaphorical way in which Spinoza's commentators extend the meaning of the term 'individual', and sometimes the metaphorical way in which even Spinoza himself treats 'bodies politic' as 'pseudo-individuals', and here the function of the expression *una veluti mente duci* is reversed (which shows not only that it 'resists' Rice's reading, but that it is likely to disturb *both* organicist and individualist schemata). The second is that Rice posits as self-evident a theoretical convergence between methodological individualism and socio-political individualism (or nominalism in philosophy and liberalism in politics). This assimilation seems to me a prejudice, typical of a certain Anglo-American tradition (though it does not have a monopoly on this). The problem is palpable here in a specific discussion of the implications of the notion of the *multitudo*, which is central to Spinoza's elaborations (especially in the *Political Treatise*), and which can of course be understood in two registers: in relation to the question of 'power' and to that of 'right'. Which brings us neatly to Antonio Negri's position.

## 3. Negri

We find similarly in Negri a systematic treatment of the problem posed by Spinoza's formula, with its double movement of the introduction and withdrawal of the transindividual analogy. There is nothing surprising about this if we remember that, for Negri, *potentia multitudinis* (a phrase that almost has the status of a redundancy, since all 'power' is always that of a multiple or a multitude, and all multiplicity is essentially a deployment of natural power) is the key concept of Spinoza's thought, one that manifests the absolute reversibility of metaphysical discourse and political discourse. It is for this very reason that Negri proposes to view the *Political Treatise* as the crowning achievement of Spinoza's metaphysics, as a 'constitution of reality', despite its incompleteness (which can be read positively, Spinoza having, in short, already said everything he had to say about democracy by the moment he had to stop, although without having written a corresponding chapter), albeit with the exception of its purely institutional discussions (which in Negri's eyes mark a relapse into the ideologies of his time).

In the detail, however, a reversal occurs between two successive versions of Negri's argument (between which he takes into account a certain number of objections), although they tend at base towards the same result. The chapter of *The Savage Anomaly* that he devotes to commentary on the *Political Treatise* has as its guiding thread the possibility of understanding all the moments of political theory, with the apparent oppositions that characterise it (the sovereign power of the state versus the freedom of the people or of society, the absoluteness versus the internal limitation of power, etc.), as developments of a single principle: the expansiveness and the capacity for self-organisation of the *multitudo* (a term that he does not generally translate, but which connotes for him the originally collective character of the political force and its *conatus* or own desire, as opposed to the methodological individualism of contract theories).[23] When he reaches the fundamental parts of Chapters 3 and 4, where the *potentia multitudinis* is characterised by the fact that it is 'directed as if by a single mind', Negri does not deal explicitly with the *veluti*, but he does implicitly propose an interpretation of it, which can be boiled down to the following three points:

1. The definition of the power of the state as *potentia multitudinis* (and the 'pure affirmation' of this power) must include *the antagonism of subjects* which explains its productivity (consistent with this, Negri counterposes its autonomy to 'juridical' representations of the state's unity).
2. The antagonistic structure of the *multitudo*, however, finds its immediate corrective in the *fear of loneliness* that originally animates the mass (*Political Treatise* 6.1) and pushes it to unite in search of security. This appears to be a negative passion, but is in reality constructive, from which the continuous growth of sociality results, without the necessary mediation of any external power imposing itself.
3. The constitution is therefore, in one and the same movement, the emergence of a *subject*, but this one is none other than, precisely, the *multitudo*, or it is as such multiple (and therefore irrepresentable in terms of power, legal personhood, institutional sovereignty, etc.).

We are, here, obviously, at the antipodes of the idea previously encountered in Matheron, without being on Rice's side: if the *una veluti mente* has a meaning, it is not to mark a gap between the real individuality of the body politic and its approximation by sovereign power, but to indicate that real power *exceeds any representation of unity*, presenting an essential ontological multiplicity (and which by the same token includes antagonism, or is nourished by it, instead of seeing it as a mortal danger).[24]

In a later text,[25] taking into consideration 'critics who have denied the importance of the *multitudo* as the subject and the central metaphysical attribution of Spinoza's doctrine of the State' in insisting on 'the elusiveness of the concept', Negri modifies the form of his argument to answer them. He tries more than ever to show that 'the material elusiveness of the subject-*multitudo* does not for Spinoza mean that effects of subjectivity are not expressed'. But it must be admitted that there is tension, even contradiction, within the very concept of *multitudo*, because, under certain conditions (those of state construction, the conscious objective of which is to *limit* the autonomous power of the mass), it must be *represented as a unity* of decision and thought: the prototype of such a representation is Rousseau's 'general will', a juridical fiction which is the keystone of the contractarian tradition of legitimation of the political state.

It is in fact at just such a fiction (an 'idea of reason', or a 'product of the imagination') that the notion of a 'quasi-spirit', or the repetition of the formula *una veluti mente ducitur*, in Spinoza's text is aimed in advance. Spinoza is trying to make the ungraspable graspable. However, the *multitudo* in itself 'remains an elusive set of singularities'. It is not a mind or a spirit, but a material historical power. And this pole remains dominant: 'reason, thought, would like the *multitudo* to be presented as a single mind: this demand of reason traverses the natural field on which social life unfolds but does not manage to overcome' it. It must then be added that the expansive (productive and creative) power of the *multitudo* manifests itself precisely through its capacity to utilise inadequate representations that reduce it to a unity, through passional mechanisms such as the *pietas* or 'desire for the universal', in the service of the collective. We are very close here, paradoxically, to a conception of a 'cunning of reason'. Even though reason strives towards the multiplicity and not the unity of the subject, this movement is posited as essentially unachieved and unachievable. It is the strength of Negri's text, even if one contests his reading, to carry this idea to its conclusion by making Spinoza's politics a philosophy of *praxis*, and by putting at its service the idea of an intrinsic aporia, affecting not theory but things themselves:

> Becoming real, in Spinoza's politics, has the power and limit of fact. . . . The non-solution of the problem of the political subject becomes the foundation of tolerance. . . . Each singularity is a foundation. . . . These conclusions, relative to the concept of the *multitudo*, do not therefore eliminate its aporetic nature; rather, they accentuate it. . . . Its concept cannot be closed off. . . . The political universe is a universe of action. The fact that democracy appears an objective aporia of the absolute and freedom, and that this aporia is posited as the dynamic condition of the political process, certainly does not resolve the problem and the difficulties of the definition of democracy, but rather aggravates it. . . . For if it is necessary to act it is necessary to do so knowing that the aporia is always present in the action: the aporia is thereby transferred from objectivity to subjectivity. The subject must act while acknowledging the non-conclusiveness of the universe in which it acts. It must act nevertheless. . . . My conjecture is that Spinozian democracy, the *omnino absolutum democraticum imperium*, must be conceived as a social practice of singularities that intersect in a mass process – or better, as a *pietas* that forms and constitutes the reciprocal individual relations that stretch between the multiplicity of subjects constituting the *multitudo*.[26]

In short, Negri's idea is that the concept of 'subject' or of 'subjectivity' has two antithetical meanings: either the unity of a *representation* (including that of a *mens* qua individual mind), or the *power to act* and ultimately *the action* itself. Spinoza, for his part, would have clearly chosen the second, even at the price of a meandering elaboration of which his discourse bears the trace. I strongly doubt that such any alternative could be Spinozist. But it brings us to the heart of the difficulties of the text of the *Political Treatise*, which concern not only political theory, but its 'foundations', which is to say metaphysics.

## *A critical solution: Moreau*

With Pierre-François Moreau's analyses, our method changes. After a series of discussions which show the crucial character of the question of the individuality of the body politic in Spinoza, he dedicates a section of his book, *Experience and Eternity in Spinoza*, to classifying the existing positions in the literature (albeit with the exception of Negri's), to placing the problem in a more general context (the articulation of the theory of passions with the theory of history, which leads to this playing a privileged role in the complementarity of the *Political Treatise* and the *Theological Political Treatise*), and to propose an original line of interpretation ('The passional root of the symbolic and its effects').[27] Without recounting all the details here, I would like to mention some salient points.

Before coming to the question of the individuality of peoples, Moreau endeavours to show that the opposition between Hobbes and Spinoza on the question of 'natural right' rests on the fact that, for Spinoza, 'the power of the passions' constitutes its effective reality. This does not mean that the foundation or construction of the state is just a matter of a game of certain passions against others. It is, rather, a matter of finding in every man 'a passionate aspiration for the benefits of reason' which teaches the usefulness of social peace, an aspiration reinforced by experience and the sovereignty of which serves to inculcate obedience to institutions. This lesson, essentially based on a reading of the *Theological Political Treatise*, must also be possible to extend to the *Political Treatise*. But experience does not just have an auxiliary function: as the result of its duration, it also appears as constitutive of the historical individuality that makes people into *a* people. It is in these terms that Moreau undertakes to solve the question of the extension of the model of individuality initially forged in relation to the singular human being to the body politic (to societies which are also states with their own institutions). His demonstration starts from an examination of the way Spinoza applies the category of *ingenium* (which he translates as *complexion*) to historical peoples (*nationes*, *gentes*). The *ingenium*, made up of acquired or historically constituted mores and beliefs, forms the equivalent of a nature, which is to say that it is absolutely singular (specific to each people), such that a system of institutions is viable only if it conforms to it. In short, it defines the natural *boundaries* between which the constitution of the state, or the form of power, operates. At the other extreme, his demonstration leads to an analysis (this time based on the *Ethics*) of the membership mechanisms that crystallise a 'collective identity' of peoples and of the subjective conditions under which the form of institutions (onto which Moreau projects, in an anachronistic but illuminating way, the modern concept of 'the symbolic order') ensures (or does not ensure) its durability. Between the two, the real discussion of the form of individuality proper to the state takes place, the main stake of which is the modality according to which it is possible to attribute to it something 'like a mind'.

The interpretation of the *veluti* or the *quasi* is at the heart of Moreau's interpretation, which concerns both Spinoza's corpus and all the interpretations to which it has given rise (in some respects taking up Claude Lefort's method in relation to Machiavelli, and thus saying that a thought is inseparable from its writing): by analogy with the human complexion, each 'people' has its own *ingenium*, and so each 'state' is, *in a certain way*, an individual. The problem would then be to know whether, in the sense it is used the 'Spinozist system', this individuality must be considered real or metaphorical, which would be to say artificial: on the one hand Matheron's thesis, on the other that of Rice. The point of contention is the question of the *conatus*: can we say of the state that it tends to be preserved in its being, and therefore in its form? It is a question of knowing whether human individuals' membership of the state causes the formation of a stable compound whose idea would constitute 'the mind', in the sense in which it is used in Part II of the *Ethics*.

While relativising some of the terms of the debate (since in Spinozism there is no such thing as artifice, or all artifice is itself natural), Moreau wants to weigh what he calls the 'elements of the case', putting toe to toe the *naturalistic logic of Spinozism*, directly projected onto the *omnia sunt animata*,[28] and the *counter-arguments of the artificialists*, essentially based on the insistence on the expression *una veluti mente*, which would connote the opposition of a logic of relations to that of the wholes and parts, and on the continuity between the thesis of the *Theological Political Treatise* (Chapters 3 and 17) – 'nature does not create peoples, but individuals' – with that of the *Political Treatise* (5.2): 'men are not born citizens but become them'. According to Moreau, these two formulae do not have the same object, or are not situated at the same level: one refers to an ontological condition, the other to a problem of the functioning of institutions. He also tends, at base, to agree formally with the defenders of 'naturalism' (Matheron), but to immediately start thinking this in a totally new way, not physicalist, but historicising or historicist. Implicitly, what he wants to say is this: in Spinoza, *'nature' is history* (including philology, historical psychology, etc.).[29]

So to his proposals for solving the problem, which comprise his longest excursion. This constitutes a remarkable effort to take Spinoza's writing seriously, and to incorporate all of his historico-political indications into at least a plausible synthesis. Moreau begins by making three preliminary points:

1. The use of the term *veluti* is not sufficient proof against the logic of the system, because Spinoza says in *Political Treatise* 3.2 that the state (*imperium*) has a *corpus* and a *mens*.[30] Now, the *corpus* is not supposed to be subject to any restriction (see *Political Treatise* 3.5). In reality, the restriction contained in the word *veluti* would *relate* to the assimilation of the soul of the state to the *sovereign* (and implicitly to the *person* of the sovereign).
2. There is indeed a *conatus* of the state, as there is of all 'things', but this characteristic term of the language of the *Ethics* is replaced in the *Political Treatise* by the dyad of *jus* and *potentia*. The problem, therefore, is not whether the state is an individual (for everything that tends to persevere in its being is one *to some degree*), but *what kind of individual* it is.
3. The relevance of this question is confirmed by the interpretation of the thesis that 'nature does not create a people': it means, according to Moreau, that, 'the state of nature'

being an abstraction, individuals are always already social, but without this generic property telling us the norm according to which they are 'socialised'. The characteristics of the state, which, in turn, affect individuals, cannot be derived from an elementary individuality.

All these remarks lead to a reformulation of the problem: what type of individuality is the state? This means asking what type of *complexity* characterises a state individuality, which is an historical individuality (which is to say a *nation*, a concept I will come back to). Individuality and complexity (Spinoza speaks of a 'very complex' individual) are by definition *equivocal* – or in any case plurivocal – categories. Moreau's thesis (like Spinoza's) thus resolutely opposes the tradition that has made the human organism qua complex of organs the *model* of political individuality.[31] But this is necessarily completely different, on the one hand inasmuch as it involves *both* individuals *and objective relations between them* (or 'institutions'), and on the other (which seems to me basically the same idea) inasmuch as the *imperium* is not immediately identified with the people (meaning *natio* or *gens* rather than *multitudo* or *populus*? Moreau sometimes benefits from the ambiguity of the French word *peuple*). There is here a 'superior complexity' that we should put in relation with the cardinal thesis of *Theological Political Treatise* and *Political Treatise*, generalised starting from Tacitus: for the state individuality, *the danger of death comes from within*, from internal conflicts. So, a political individual never 'dies' in the same way as a human body.

Here, Moreau makes a strange leap. Drawing on the Axiom of Part IV of the *Ethics,* which posits the superiority of the external forces of destruction over every individuality, he turns it inside out like a glove to make it say: *this external superiority takes on the appearance of an internal cause* 'since it proceeds by the destruction of their unity' (that of individuals, or their bodies). The question of the specificity of the political individual then becomes: why, according to what modalities (generally imaginary), does this type of natural individuality *seem to us artificial* (that is, since 'we' are always the citizens of a state, why does it seem artificial to members of the state?). If we accept this reformulation, Moreau's 'solution' is very brilliant. It proceeds by superimposing three mechanisms of socialisation, which he calls *association*, *integration* and *adhesion*, making it possible to define in the final analysis the type of collective individuality that the *imperium* among other things (religious sects, etc.) forms.

From the idea of *association*, it must be inferred that a historico-social individuality is based, unlike an organism, not on the difference and the complementarity of the parts (correlative of a high degree of *consciousness* for the mind), but on the *similarity* of its components united by a relation of *convenientia*. Here Moreau refers in turn to the Scholium to Proposition 18 of *Ethics* Part IV. He takes from this the idea of weakness or weak distinctness of the state's *mens*, while the *mentes* of the citizens continue to clash. The constitutive problem of the state is to reinforce its own *mens*, creating the *unanimity* (*animorum unio*) that the expression *una veluti mente duci* would precisely designate. This is the primordial task of policies that the organicist imaginary of the state covers with its veil of illusion.

From the idea of *integration*, which he associates with the principle of reciprocal utility, Moreau draws the idea that the citizen's mind must be identified with that of the state by various means, the most effective of which are those that take on *the appearance of reason*, in particular the collectivisation of hatreds and fears (*Political Treatise* 8.6). Such would be the function of institutions, which encourage the satisfaction of common needs by silencing mutually irreducible desires.

Finally, from the idea of *adhesion*, crowning this construction, essentially intended to show how a state can construct a simulacrum of rationality *in the imaginary*, but which will tendentially produce the same effects (that is to say, the practical recognition of the common interest), Moreau maintains that there must be *mechanisms of recognition* leading the individual to 'positively represent its relation to the totality' and to prefer subjection to the state to foreign slavery and reciprocal hatreds. It is here that he evokes in its turn the proximity of Spinoza to Machiavelli and, in a bold leap, offers as a Spinozist thesis the claim that the means of 'bringing a state back to its' original (therefore necessarily imaginary) principle consist in the *symbolism of the identity* of each national tradition, whose emblems and collective rites (the plait of the Chinese, the circumcision of the Jews) are installed as fetishes at the heart of the *ingenium* characteristic of the people, which individualises it. Or, better yet, they are installed at the heart of the correspondence between the *ingenium* of the people and that of the state (is this both the people's and the state's 'mind'? Let us call it, rather, in anachronistic but illuminating terms, the 'unconscious' of each).

This resolution of the problem, which surely borrows a certain number of elements from its predecessors, seems to me henceforth unavoidable. The emphasis on the historico-anthropological dimension of Spinoza's thought seems absolutely right to me. It does not satisfy me fully, however, because I see four possible directions from which objections may be made:

1. The resolution seems to have an element of circularity. Moreau starts from the idea that, according to Spinoza,

there exists a *popular ingenium*, and in the end he finds in the notion of this *ingenium* and its modes of expression the solution of the problem. The question of the theoretical (or systemic) consistency of the concept of *ingenium* (and especially its articulation with the concepts of mind and body) remains obscure.

2. Moreau journeys between considering ideas of an *ingenium* of the state, of the people and of the nation. My initial intuition is that these terms basically designate the same thing. At the end of the day, Moreau takes the focal point of the problem to be the formation of a more or less stable relation or a historic 'encounter' of the *ingenium* of the people with the *ingenium* of the state. But the former presupposes knowing what the unity of the *multitudo* is, and the latter seems to me impossible to find in Spinoza, or, more exactly, I do not see what the *ingenium* of the *imperium* could be of other than that of a historically organised multitude. For the same reason, I do not see how the 'composition' of individualities and the operation of 'institutions' form two different aspects of the 'complexity' studied.

3. Moreau ultimately aims to completely reduce the question of the sense in which a body politic constitutes *one* individuality of a certain type to the question of how it constitutes *a particular* singular individuality in history. But these are not the same thing (they are, rather, respectively individuation and individualisation), or at least it would be necessary to problematise their identification (pushing at the limit towards an absolute historical nominalism that there are no political 'regimes', every nation or people 'inventing' a *sui generis* political regime, unless it is itself its product: the difficulties that will result from this for reading the *Political Treatise* are

obvious). Note here that, as much as the question of *national identity* and its relation to religious identity is central in the *Theological Political Treatise*, it is marginal in the *Political Treatise*, where it is *political* identity that counts. Moreau speaks as if, counterposing Spinoza to Hobbes on the basis of current discussions, he had differentiated their problematics as that of *sovereignty* (Hobbes) and that of the relationship between *citizenship and nationality* (Spinoza). The *veluti una mente* would signify this transformation.

4. Between the two forms of 'constitution of the city' found in Part IV of the *Ethics* (and in particular in Proposition 37, with its double series of demonstrations and scholia), which form a sort of 'intra-associative parallelism', Moreau totally privileges the *passional way*. For him, the 'rationality' of the state or of the organisation of the multitude is in fact the appearance produced by an implementation or manipulation of the passions (which he calls 'symbolic'). As a result, of course, he places the entire weight of his endeavour on the 'sociological' dimensions of the problem of the *animorum unio*, tending to eliminate or ignore any *ontological* dimension. I fear that, under these conditions, the strictly 'ethical' point of view disappears.

## For a 'literalist' solution

Taking up the term 'literalism' introduced into the discussion by Lee J. Rice, and some of the elements proposed so far (but rectifying at the same time things that seems to me to force the sense of Spinoza's text), I would like to attempt a solution based on the following principles:

1. *All* occurrences of the expression *una veluti mente ducitur* (*ducuntur*) must be taken into account, regardless of the 'subject' to which it applies.[32] It follows from this that the equivocity on which many interpreters have foundered – sometimes the 'quasi-*mens*' belongs to the whole state (upon which it confers the 'power of the multitude'), sometimes to a particular institution in the state (which appropriates this power), and which presents itself differently depending on the regime – is itself this part of the problem.
2. All references to a social, political or institutional *corpus* must be taken into account, but *only* those references.[33] It follows from this that the expression *corpus imperii* is in fact as problematic as *mens civitatis*, etc. More precisely, it must be admitted that the notion of a 'body politic' coming from a tradition that is at once legal, religious and philosophical has an 'ideological' rather than a theoretical meaning in Spinoza. Its connection with a theory (a physics or an ontology) of *corporeal individuality* is therefore a problem, not a solution or a clear starting point.
3. The expression *una veluti mente duci* must systematically be compared with the other expressions which involve *ducere* and *ductus* (primarily in the *Political Treatise* but possibly elsewhere), in particular *ratione duci*, *ex ratione ductu* (*convenire*) etc. It follows that *a veluti mente ducitur* (*ducuntur*) refers by definition not to a univocal situation, but to counterposed tendencies: either the *animorum unio* (*Political Treatise* 3.7) is realised by a purely passional mechanism (fear of the law, hatred of the foreigner, hope of the common salvation, etc.), or it is realised with a view to rational utility (and by means of its representation, which does not exclude a mobilisation of passions, a point to which I will return). Here we find

ourselves meeting again, in a particular way (another point to which I will have to return), the 'double way' of constructing the concept of sociability presented in Part IV of the *Ethics*, particularly in the remarkable passage constituted by Proposition 37 with its two demonstrations and its two scholia.[34]

4. It is necessary to compare that expression with its obvious antithesis in the *Political Treatise*, which is *ex suo ingenio vivere*. It follows from this that a contradiction in Spinoza's terms in fact covers another, more decisive one. There is a *formal opposition*, in the first degree, between the unity (of thought, and therefore of decision) of the *imperium* and the 'natural' independence of individual *ingenia*, but more profoundly there is a *substantial opposition*, even within the *multitudo* (which here covers both the *imperium* and the human individuals with their own *ingenia*), between two regimes of autonomy, in truth each as paradoxical as the other. In one of these, the 'right' of each (*sui juris esse*) refers to an *ex suo ingenio vivere* which is in fact self-destructive, and therefore practically 'impossible'; in the other, this 'right' (formally identically always referred to as *sui juris esse*) incorporates the possibility of the *ex suo ingenio vivere* into a communal right, thus into the common power realised in communal life, which means, apparently, depriving it of any non-virtual content.

On the basis of these preliminary principles, we can then infer a series of consequences, by combining the ideas that have appeared. Taking the consequences of principles 3 and 4 together, it follows that the constitution of a collective *mens* is, for Spinoza, never anything in its essence other than the practical realisation of an *animorum unio*, in other words a conciliation or a combination of *ingenia*, which implies the following:

1. *All the 'degrees'* of union between the movement of passionate opinion of a crowd (for example at an insurrectionary conjuncture)[35] and rational collective deliberation in a framework of stable institutions are virtually included in the thesis of the *animorum unio*.[36] In any case, a process of thought (and of formation or transformation of thought, therefore of ideas – it is here that Appuhn's translation is interesting) is at work, but this process is by definition 'transindividual', and its object is precisely the way in which the more or less organised multitude 'perceives' itself (its interests, its composition, its divisions and its situation in the world) and thus perceives itself to be 'organised'.
2. However, this process of thought is not so much 'ideal' or purely 'spiritual' (or even 'deliberate' in its essence, even if it does involve moments of deliberation). What the insistent reference to *ingenia* connotes is, on the contrary, the fact that it reflects and articulates the power of the bodies of which the multitude is composed and their singularity, their particular 'way of life' (which Cristofolini's translation expresses well: *a modo suo vivere*).[37]
3. The collective *mens* is therefore by definition a *quasi mens* (as indicated at *Ethics* Part VI, Proposition 18, Scholium), the *unity-of-conduct* of which is thinkable only in the mode of 'as if'. Not that it is not 'mental' (which is to say ideal or thinking), but its direction is unified (and therefore 'defined') only tendentially (one could say 'asymptotically' to reason and communal utility), and therefore itself is unified only tendentially – in a *precarious* way, one might say – because in Spinoza a *mens* cannot be anything other than the organised whole of 'its' ideas. In fact, it is its own ability to conduct or direct (*ducere*) in a univocal way that unites it, conferring on

it an internal 'order' (the order of ideas in which it consists), and thus making it exist. A disorganised *mens*, without unity of any kind, would actually barely exist.[38]

But all this, in turn, has an effect on the implications we have drawn from principle 2 concerning the use and meaning of the word 'body' in Spinoza: to think of the 'body' politic or the individuality of the body politic as something that pre-exists the constitution of the quasi-*mens* (or to the quasi-constitution of the *mens*, which is to say of the *animorum unio*) is radically excluded as a possibility and this would come to be reflected after the fact. The 'body' politic is, rather, contrary to this mechanistic representation, the effect of the unification of the *mens*, as tendentious and precarious as it is (even if, obviously, one must posit a *threshold* for its formation, its coming into existence, something I have called elsewhere after Deleuze an 'incompressible minimum').[39] This is to say again — we are here at the heart of the critical relationship with Hobbes – that the term 'body politic' does not stipulate anything by itself. Or, rather, it reflects the ambition of the state (of the *imperium* in its different forms) to integrate, unify and incorporate the *potentia multitudinis* into its own 'life', an ambition which is 'in itself' rational and in accordance with the common good, the common interest, but which will be realised more or less well according to the nature of the regime.

One could thus draw this conclusion: without a *minimum* of communal thought and therefore a minimum of incorporation, there would be no state at all (or, if you like, there would be only a contradictory and self-destructive *multitudo*). But the question then arises of where there is, conversely, a *maximum*. One might be tempted to say that it is the absolute unification of the thought-of-the-masses, a 'single thought' in which individual differences, which are so many virtual contradictions, would be completely absorbed or melt into what Matheron calls a *consensus*, a 'conformism'. However, it is not. On the contrary, such a hypothesis returns us to the *minimum*, and perhaps below the *minimum*. Here one must use the *Theological Political Treatise*, which deals with precisely this question, to complete the *Political Treatise*. The attempt to homogenise different thoughts by abolishing their singularity (whether in the form of a *theologico-political credo*, as is perpetuated in absolute monarchy, or in that of a *myth of reason*, as is presented in enlightened despotism and in a certain 'republican' tradition) is ultimately doomed to failure. But before collapsing it can – as we know and Spinoza never ceased to worry – generate the worst violence, the dissociation of the community.[40] It does not in fact represent a real synthesis, a *universalisation* of opinions and ways of life, but the vain attempt of a particular ambition to incorporate all others. We must therefore adopt the opposite position: there is *no maximum* of 'communal thought', precisely because communal thought develops towards infinity in the sense of the highest possible compatibility of the most elevated possible singularities (in *Spinoza and Politics*, I called this being 'as many as possible, thinking as much as possible', referring to the *Ethics* Part V, Propositions 5–10).[41]

To finish these interpretative hypotheses reflecting on our first principle, concerning the diffusion of the uses of the expression *una mente ducitur*, what we have seen is that the 'subject' imputed in this action – or, better yet, in this dynamic process in which activity and passivity consist – 'being directed as by one mind', literally *fluctuates* between the whole and the part, between the *multitudo* and the *imperium*, and even between the *imperium* and the *summae potestates*. These are all terms which, in a sense, mean the same thing (that is, they express only modalities of the same *conatus*, the same *res*) and in another sense continue to dissociate from or even oppose each other. In view of the foregoing, it must of course be ruled out, in my view, that there is a hesitation in Spinoza as to the question of *where to locate* the unity of the body politic or social individuality. Such a hesitation could only emanate from an essentialist point of view, which he has renounced. On the contrary, it must be asserted that the *limits of this individuality* themselves fluctuate, between a 'totalisation' and a 'separation', the latter having the double sense of a scission in society (*civitas*) and of an isolation of the sovereign. One could say again that it is the *potentia multitudinis* which is sometimes fully 'internalised', applying itself in its totality to itself, sometimes 'externalised' or containing within itself a point of exception, applying itself only to a part of itself, as if from without, like the action of a coercive state power that wants to 'represent' to the mass of the people a unity of which it by itself is incapable.

But we know that this fluctuation is endless, although it is traversed by an ethical or ethico-political orientation or *effort* (which also corresponds to a 'duty' – see the use by Spinoza in some of the quoted passages of the verb *debere*). The consequence for the identity of the 'political subject' is that it is, indeed, as Negri says – but for quite different reasons to his – 'ungraspable' or, better yet, *equivocal*. It is impossible to locate it *either in the whole or in the part*, which is to say either in the 'people' or in the 'state'. If, therefore, *multitudo* designates *par excellence* the popular authority on which the power of the state and its stability or instability depend, it is not possible strictly to say that the subject *is the multitudo*, except by specifying immediately that this be at the price of insoluble contradictions, in the form of an infinite regression, etc. But if, conversely, *multitudo* designates precisely a contradictory unity – fluctuating according to regimes and situations in line with the model of the *fluctuatio animi* (and perhaps I should venture the expression *fluctatio mentis*) – of the *imperium* and the *populus* (or the *demos*), which, each in its own way, may claim to embody or represent the political 'subject', then we must admit that this subject is as such paradoxical, or that it is a *non-subject*, in relation to classical conceptions.

The reversal of the classical figure of the subject leads in particular to a radical contrast between the Spinozian conception of politics – the metaphysics of politics in Spinoza – and that of Hobbes as much as that of Rousseau. Not (as Negri would have it) because Hobbes and Rousseau share the same conception, but on the contrary because, opposing one another, they illustrate the two possibilities of conferring on the 'body politic' the unity of a classical subject, either as a transcendent unity or as an immanent unity. It is not to say, however (I will grant Negri this), that the reversal excludes forms and practices of *subjectivation*. On the contrary, it is a way of understanding why politics (and history as a political scene) is never anything other than a field of subjective movements: activity and passivity, increase and decrease of the power to act, composition or *convenientia* and decomposition of collective individualities or *seditio*. But we have no reason – quite the contrary, going by the whole Spinozist analysis of the modalities of the *conatus* – to decide unilaterally that *one of these vectors* represents subjectivity 'in itself'.

## Provisional conclusion

I have tried to give a theoretical status to the idea of a 'quasi *mens*', evoked in passing in the *Ethics*, in the context of an analysis of the passage from individuality to transindividuality, suggesting that the *Political Treatise* develops this, and focusing on the expression *una veluti mente duci* as the key to understanding this development. A 'quasi *mens*' – if this expression can be sustained – corresponds in my account to the idea of a 'transindividual' *mens*, and more precisely to what a mental identity for a transindividual composite would be, if precisely such a composite were not situated at the limit of application of the concept of individuality and if it were not in fact a question of a *quasi-individual* rather than of a given and completed 'individuality'. Starting from this hypothesis of a *limit-concept*, it remains, then, to try to measure its import for Spinozism in general. I will do this by following two paths of generalisation.

One would be to return to the problem of the *mens* in its generality, reflecting on this fact: the extension of this concept beyond the limits of Spinoza's first use of it – broadly the one at the centre of the demonstrations of the *Ethics*, linking the analysis of the passional and rational movements of the human mind, defined as an idea of the multiplicity proper to the human body, to a general problematic of the attributes of substance and its expression according to these attributes – has made us discover a quasi-psyche or, better yet, an almost individual psyche (because it is the very same elements that go into the formation of the individual human *mens* – what Spinoza calls 'ideas' – and these ideas correspond to movements and bodily encounters, but within a broader framework). This is a matter of a transindividual regime of production and association of ideas, which tends towards unity only to the extent that it is compatible with a degree of complexity and conflictuality superior to that of human individuality – the political field illustrates this – and which coincides with its own singularity.

The common thread that I would like to follow is both historical and philological. It would be a matter of starting from the axiomatic statement *omnia sunt animata*,[42] and of exploring its transformation by following, on the one hand, Emilia Giancotti's suggestion: in the development of Spinozism, references to the *anima* and to the idea of an *animatio* of the body have been tendentially eliminated in favour of what can be considered a radicalisation of Cartesianism, which is to say an extension of the analysis of the passions to the logic of ideas, specifically referring to the word *mens*.[43] This means, clearly, both that all affects are radically intellectualised and that all ideas, including the most adequate ones, are inseparable from affective modalities, or realisations of desire. But we must also follow Pierre-François Moreau's suggestion that the term *ingenium*, even if it is subject only to a 'practical use' (as Althusser would have said), contains the key to the problem of *the identity of individuals*, and so also to that of collective quasi-individualities. That said, what seems to me to play the decisive role in the most sophisticated version of Spinozist thought on this point is not the designation of an *ingenium* of peoples or nations (which I am also not far from considering to be a 'quasi *ingenium*', at least if it must be understood as a 'natural kind' persisting through history),[44] but, rather, the relation between the formation of transindividual ideas (the socio-political content of which we know to be the unification of common opinions and mass notions, the formation in action of a thought of the multitude) and the *ingenium* of each one.

I am, then, tempted to retranslate this term, not just as 'complexion', 'natural kind' or 'personality',[45] but as *resistance to assimilation*: a resistance belonging to the individual psyche, rooted in the psycho-physical complex. And my (provisional) hypothesis is that the Spinozist identification of affective processes with intellectual processes (or ideals) in the concept of the *mens* in a way leaves a 'remainder', which is precisely what the term *ingenium* designates. *In addition to* the concept of a *mens*, in order to analyse what the movements of bodies in the attribute of 'thought' correspond to, and especially to analyse the forms of attraction and repulsion between individualities that is produced there, the concept or quasi-concept of an *ingenium* is required. This emerges in its irreducible function from the extension of an ethical problem, that of transindividual combinations, to the political field, but it doubtless has a more general scope. Or perhaps it would be better to say: its centrality reflects the fact that *all* mental processes, if 'individualised', always already have a transindividual dimension.

But here we come to the other path along which I envisage generalising the foregoing questions. I believe that the discussions that I have surveyed or initiated raise a double difficulty. On the one hand, they continually confront us with a transgression of the rules of correspondence between attributes, commonly designated by the name of 'parallelism' – or what I think I understand by this name at least. We first encountered this, while following the very letter of the *Political Treatise*, in Spinoza's surprising logical 'weakness' in not positing an identity in the difference between the bodily individuality and mental individuality of the state, but rather – at least in the case of the monarchy – an action of the *imperium* (identified with a 'mind') on the *multitudo* or the *civitas* (identified with a 'body'). And this continued by way of the hypothesis to which I myself have been led by a state constitution that is a 'quasi *corpus*' as a consequence of its constitution in a 'quasi *mens*'. What should we make of these paradoxes? Should we see them as proof of Spinozism's inconsistency in relation to its own premises as soon as it enters the terrain of politics? Or, on the contrary, should we seize on this and try to put it to the test, and if necessary modify our understanding of the axiom of the parallelism of the attributes and causal substance, as if the *Ethics* had not already explored this and elucidated all its aspects?

In my opinion, these questions are not separable from the problem posed profoundly by Moreau,[46] which I have tried to reformulate by means of the category of the 'transindividual': no doubt there is a general concept of individuality and individuation in Spinoza, which also applies to the production of the effects of substance (in the last analysis, it is in fact *individualities*, singular things, which are both causes and effects, which produce and which are produced). But it is profoundly mistaken to represent *all* processes of individuation on the model of *human* individuation (that of the body and the individual human mind). This is precisely anthropomorphic illusion, the fundamental structure of the imaginary, which has a privileged place in the representation of political phenomena – if need be by way of a theological anthropomorphism, as seen in Hobbes's 'Mortall God'. But the analysis of political phenomena, in turn, is the royal road to a critique of this illusion. It presents us with a limit-individuality (quasi-individuality or transindividuality) which also concerns bodies and souls, physical movements and associations of ideas, but obeys a completely different model. If it turns out that, in fact, this transindividual dimension is also *always already* implicated in the life of human individuality, especially in the movement of its passions, that it always *overdetermines* it, as Parts III and IV of the *Ethics* more than suggest, there would be – via politics – a fundamental indication of the fact that, for Spinoza, the great philosophical challenge is to *think man out of all anthropomorphism*, that is to say, to liberate oneself as a theoretician (or should we say as a 'sage'?) from all the *models* that man (which is to say, the multitude of men) unceasingly assigns to himself.

## Notes

1 The comma written by Carl Gebhardt (*Spinoza Opera*, 4 vols, Heidelberg, 1924) between 'corpus' and 'et mens' was deleted in the Bartuschat edition. Cristofolini indicates that the word 'sicuti', missing in the *Opera posthuma*, is a correction by the editors. See: Carl Gebhardt, *Spinoza Opera* (4 vols) (Heidelberg: Carl Winter Verlag, 1924); Baruch de Spinoza, *Politischer Traktat. Lateinisch-Deutsch*, trans. Wolfgang Bartuschat (Hamburg: Felix Meiner Verlag, 1994); Baruch Spinoza, *Trattato politico*, trans. Paolo Cristofolini (Pisa: Edizioni ETS, 1999).
2 Edwin Curley, *The Collected Works of Spinoza*, Volume II: 2 (Princeton: Princeton University Press, 2016), p. 517. Translator's note: in the French original, Balibar lists only three translations, not including the English, providing Curley's English rendering rather only in a footnote after the third, German translation. Obviously, the English version is indispensable to our purposes so I have given it the pride of second place previously accorded to the French, even though Balibar does not discuss this translation.
3 Pierre-François Moreau, in Spinoza, *Tractatus politicus. Traité Politique* (Paris: Réplique, 1979), pp. 33–5.
4 Spinoza, *Trattato politico*, trans. Cristofolini, p. 55.
5 Spinoza, *Politischer Traktat*, trans. Bartuschat, p. 35.
6 Spinoza, *Trattato Politico*, trans. Cristofolini, p. 245, note.
7 'Man, I say, can wish for nothing more helpful to the preservation of his being than that all should so agree in all things that the Minds and Bodies of all would compose, as it were, one Mind and one Body; that all should strive together, as far as they can, to preserve their being.'

8   Most translators have agreed perfectly with this, re-establishing the *quasi* as a 'common factor', hence Bernard Pautrat's 'en sorte que les Esprits et les Corps de tous composent pour ainsi dire un seul Esprit et un seul Corps', Emilia Giancotti's 'in modo tale che le Menti e i Corpi di tutti compongano quasi una sola Mente e un solo Corpo', and Bartuschat's 'nichts Geeigneteres . . . als dass alle in allem so übereinstimmten, dass die Geister und die Körper von allen zusammen gleichsam einen einzigen Geist und einen einzigen Körper bilden'.

9   *Political Treatise* 8.19: 'It's necessary that all the Patricians be so bound by the laws that they compose, as it were, one body, governed by one mind'.

10  To which we should here add again the *Political Treatise* 6.19, concerning the monarchy: 'et absolute Rex censendus est veluti Civitatis mens, hoc autem Consilium mentis sensus externi, seu Civitate corpus, per quod mens Civitatis statum concipit, et per quod mens id agit, quod sibi optimum esse decernit'.

11  Matheron dispenses with this confusing formula by deeming it 'inopportune', but he nonetheless inserts it into an argument intended to distinguish the Hobbesian and Spinozist uses of the concept of individuality or of the 'body' politics from one another; A. Matheron, *Individu et communauté chez Spinoza* (Paris: Éditions de Minuit, 1969), p. 347 note 152.

12  In point of fact, Moreau is preoccupied essentially with the first two of these interpretations, and attaches no particular importance to Negri's.

13  'The right of the supreme powers is determined by their power, and we've seen that [that right] consists chiefly in this, that it is, as it were, the mind of the state, by which everyone ought to be guided.'

14  'That is . . . also the body and mind of the whole state.'

15  Laurent Bove, *La stratégie du conatus. Affirmation et résistance chez Spinoza* (Paris: Vrin, 1996), pp. 241–54.

16  Christian Lazzeri, *Droit, pouvoir et liberté. Spinoza critique de Hobbes* (Paris: Presses universitaires de France, 1998), pp. 280–4.

17  A. Matheron, 'L'indignation et le conatus de l'Etat spinoziste', in M. Revault d'Allonnes and H. Rizk (eds), *Spinoza: puissance et ontologie* (Paris: Éditions Kimé, 1994), pp. 153–65.

18  Lee J. Rice, 'Individual and community in Spinoza's social psychology', in Edwin Curley and Pierre-François Moreau (eds), *Spinoza: Issues and Directions. The Proceedings of the Chicago Spinoza Conference* (Leiden: E. J. Brill, 1990), pp. 271–85.

19  Rice addends to this critique some interesting remarks that cannot fail to interest anyone who has struggled with the difficulty of interpreting

Spinoza's 'physics' in relation to the history of science and of understanding its function in the rational order of the *Ethics*, where it figures parenthetically and is never explicitly taken up subsequently. On the first point, he rails against reading 'oscillation' or 'undulation' as corpuscular, as in the interpretation of Spinoza's physics advanced by Jonathan Bennett (as Spinoza's 'field metaphysic'). On the second point, he goes so far as to suggest that Spinoza brackets this discussion because he cannot really demonstrate the 'correspondence' between thought processes and bodily processes that his 'psychophysical parallelism' postulates.

20 Which is to say that this is how Rice understands them, of course, which is, then, how the liberal individualist tradition critically views them.

21 It is undoubtedly significant that the proponents of the 'organicist' interpretation tend to foreground the *passional genesis* of the Spinozist city (Matheron speaks of a 'theory of the passions of the body politic', even if he in no way ignores the duality of perspectives in the *Ethics*), whereas the advocates of the 'individualist' interpretation tend to privilege its *rational genesis*, especially in the sense of its logic of utility. We will find this problem recurring in Moreau, who from this point of view leans clearly towards the former camp. As for Negri, he succeeds in the feat of arguing that, for Spinoza, the true name of reason is 'imagination' (cleaving close on this point to the way Deleuze interprets 'active affects').

22 N. Goodman, *Of Mind and Other Matters* (Cambridge, MA: Harvard University Press, 1984).

23 A. Negri, *The Savage Anomaly: The Power of Spinoza's Metaphysics and Politics* (Minneapolis: University of Minnesota Press, 1991), ch. 8, 'The constitution of reality', in particular pp. 191–210.

24 This is also why, in his reconstruction of the movement which, by his lights, pushes Spinoza's thought towards its own clarification, Negri privileges the *Political Treatise* (or at least its first part) in relation to the *Ethics*: he sees in it the definitive reversal of the orientation towards unity in favour of an orientation towards multiplicity (implying the primacy of 'modes' over 'substance' in their constitutive relation).

25 '*Reliqua desiderantur*: a conjecture for a definition of the concept of democracy at the final Spinoza', in *Subversive Spinoza: (Un)contemporary Variations* (Manchester: Manchester University Press, 2004), pp. 28–58.

26 Ibid., p. 45.

27 P.-F. Moreau, *Spinoza. L'expérience et l'éternité* (Paris: Presses universitaires de France, 1994), ch. 3, section 3: 'L'*ingenium* du peuple et l'âme de l'État', pp. 427–65.

28 But without thematising here the question of the *anima–mens* relation, which, we shall see, is in fact closely linked to the status of the words *quasi* and *veluti*.
29 This asymmetrical tendency of Moreau's 'critical solution' has an interesting result: the form in which it tends to take up some of the suggestions of the 'artificialists' consists in a reinterpretation from within of 'naturalism'. For example, what Rice calls 'relations', of which he always emphasises the 'contingency', become in Moreau the 'institutions', which must be taken into account in relation to the composition of bodies politic *as well as* of individuals, and of which he emphasises the 'historical' character.
30 Surprisingly, Moreau, who is interested alternately in the two parts of the crucial phrase (*Political Treatise* 3.2), never really discusses the syntax and rhetoric of the sequence as I have tried to do above.
31 In his commentary on Part II of the *Ethics*, Macherey defends a similar position, starting from a 'minimalist' reading of the 'treatise on bodies' inserted after Proposition 13. Pierre Macherey, *Introduction à l'Ethique de Spinoza. La quatrième partie: la condition humaine* (Paris: Presses universitaires de France, 1997).
32 Barring error or omission: *Political Treatise* 2.16–17; 2.21; 3.1–2; 3.5; 3.7; 4.1–2; 6.1; 6.19; 8.6; 8.19. To which may be added 9.14 (*veluti corpus*) and 10.1 (*sicuti humano corpori*).
33 In his translation of the *Political Treatise*, influenced by the terminology of the 'body politic' in classic authors, Moreau uses this term more widely (for example to translate *civitas*).
34 I have shown elsewhere, how this two-sided proposition organises the whole of Part IV of the *Ethics*. Étienne Balibar, *Spinoza and Politics* (London: Verso, 1998), pp. 77–87.
35 Or indeed the 'democratic lynching' of which Matheron speaks.
36 Here I pay special attention to the store that Spinoza places in a thesis he draws from Aristotle and Machiavelli: the proliferation of different opinions expressed in collective deliberation and leading to a majority resolution of conflicts is a guarantee of rationality and wisdom (*Political Treatise* 4.4, 7.4–7, etc.). I commented on this in *Spinoza and Politics*, pp. 72–4, and in 'Spinoza, the anti-Orwell: the fear of the masses', in *Masses, Classes, Ideas* (New York: Routledge, 1994), pp. 3–37.
37 See also on this point Warren Montag's remarkable discussions in his book *Bodies, Masses, Power: Spinoza and His Contemporaries* (London: Verso 1999), in particular pp. 62ff., 'The body of the multitude'.
38 One might ask whether this would not be, at the other extreme, a

borderline case, as paradoxical as that of *corpora simplicissima* in Cristofolini's interpretation of it, to which I would agree.
39  Balibar, 'Spinoza, the anti-Orwell', pp. 33ff.
40  Does this mean that in reality – in accordance with the classical tradition descending from Plato and Aristotle – *anarchy and tyranny are not two distinct situations?*
41  Balibar, *Spinoza and Politics*, p. 98.
42  Or, to be very precise: 'Individua . . . omnia, quamvis diversis gradibus animata tamen sunt' (*Ethics* Part II, Proposition 13, Scholium).
43  Emilia Giancotti Boscherini, 'Sul concetto spinoziano di *Mens*', in Giovanni Crapulli and Emilia Giancotti Boscherini, *Ricerche lessicali su opere di Descartes e Spinoza*, Lessico Intellettuale Europeo III (Rome: Edizioni dell'Ateneo, 1969).
44  Without this, there will be very little means, at least at the descriptive level, of distinguishing Spinoza from a representative of the 'psychology of peoples' and of their distinctive 'character' or 'spirit'.
45  In German, Manfred Walther offers *Eigensinn*, which seems to me also to introduce a very interesting problematic; in any case, it is an extraordinarily polysemic notion, which does not contradict – far from it – the function of the 'remainder' or 'supplement' I talk about here.
46  See also Pierre Macherey's remarks in his commentary on Part II of the *Ethics* on the status of the small treatise on the 'physics of the body', which I will have to revisit in detail. Macherey, *Introduction*. And above all, one should take into account François Zourabichvili's analyses in the first of two published volumes of his thesis, *Spinoza: Une physique de la pensée* (Paris: Presses universitaires de France, 2002).

# 4

# Philosophies of the Transindividual: Spinoza, Marx, Freud

The lecture I gave in 1993 to the Spinozahuis Society in Rijnsburg, later published under the title *Spinoza: From Individuality to Transindividuality* (an updated version of which appears here as Chapter 1), seems to have in part been the point of origin of a sustained interest, in several languages, in the meaning and possible uses in philosophy, politics and the social sciences of the category of the 'transindividual', evinced by several recent publications.[1] This was due in particular, I think, to the rapprochement that I effected between a characteristic of Spinoza's thought that sets it apart in the history of classical ontology, which had already been identified under a different name by some commentators (in particular Alexandre Matheron), and the terminology chosen by a contemporary philosopher, then little known and recognised, Gilbert Simondon, who made it the pivot of his own system, hoping for a simultaneous transformation of modes of thinking about nature and culture. The situation has since evolved greatly, above all else because Simondon's thought has become a 'major' philosophical reference, crossing borders and becoming the object of numerous studies.

We must credit this to the posthumous publication of numerous pieces, as well as to the multiplication of discussions of his work, in the first rank of which – following on from the praise lavished on it by Deleuze – we must place Muriel Combes's work. We should also credit the increase in the network of analogies and affinities between Simondon's idea of the transindividual, centred on *individuation* as a universal ontological and morphological category, applicable to all kinds of beings, and the objectives of a contemporary philosophy of *becoming*, of collective *transformation*, of the *plasticity* of institutions, casting suspicion again on metaphysical oppositions between the reign of necessity and that of freedom. For Simondon, in contrast to the 'hylomorphic scheme' that dominates the whole history of Western philosophy, even among nominalist thinkers, the individual form is neither the goal nor the model according to which a *formation* of the individual should be regulated. It is only the unstable result (or, better, in the terminology of the thermodynamics of systems, the 'metastable' state, which is to say the state between *thresholds* of aggregation and disaggregation) of a process that is in itself infinite. Simondon's individuation occupies an intermediate position between a 'pre-individual' potential that it expresses but never exhausts, and a 'transindividual' excess in which it is always already engaged. And on the other hand, it must be thought as the singular, momentary state of a *relation* or a set of relations, at once internal and external, the terms of which do not pre-exist it, since they themselves have to be individualised.

It is because of these characteristics, which transgress the established philosophical order, and not only because of his terminological innovation (even though the two things are closely related), that I sought in Simondon an inspiration and a support in my attempt to re-read Spinoza and Marx (or rather *part* of Spinoza and of Marx) together under the rubric of an 'ontology of relations' (and of the ontological primacy of relations as such).[2] Without losing all I have gained from this, I would like now nonetheless to explore, in parallel, another way, if only so as not to give the impression – in my opinion misleading – that transindividuality constitutes the *object*, identified unequivocally, from which one could now assemble a whole philosophical 'family', when it is, rather, a case, in the beginning, of a programmatic name clothing a sort of *via negativa* leading out of the metaphysics of the subject and of substance, and opening onto multiple, perhaps mutually contradictory possible interpretations. But I will invoke two more precise reasons for not dealing with Simondon here. The first is that Simondon's conception takes up an antinomy (recognised by his better interpreters)[3] in relation to the idea of *nature*. This would have to allow simultaneously thinking an increasing complexity of 'phases', with the human order emerging from the physical and vital 'incomplete' orders which precede it, together with the disposition to the collective which, specifically, is immanent to human relations. One can ask oneself whether there is not here a simple transposition of the classical antinomy of determinism and freedom, but in any case this difficulty calls for a critical solution. The second reason is that Simondon (and even more so his readers) generally refuses to situate himself on the terrain of *philosophical anthropology* in order to analyse relationality as such, that which constitutes the *social* that one talks about when one speaks of 'social relations', not simply as another name or a doublet of originary communal being, but as a problem to which diverse societies, historical moments and antagonistic political configurations come up with solutions which are always irreducible to a single principle. One thus risks starting from individuation thought as a process and not from the completed individual, returning to the metaphysical antithesis of the individual and the collective which we had sought to escape. And, above all, there is a lack of critical mediation between the discourse of ontology and that of politics, creating the risk that the connection between them will fluctuate between one of normative *foundation* and an anarchic *indeterminacy*: *a single political norm* that is deduced 'ontologically', or *an arbitrary norm* without comparative criteria.

I do not conclude from this that the idea of an 'ontology of relations', which I myself make use of, is absurd or useless – especially if one continues to take heed of the semantic paradox it contains (since ontology means by definition a doctrine of *being*, of which relations are only the correlate). But I do infer from this that it may be advantageous, at this stage of exploring and of constructing a new 'grammar' for philosophy, to incorporate into its categories the political presupposition that they seek to generalise and the statement of which they are meant to problematise, to return once again to the comparative examination of *classical* discourses that have explored different ways of re-establishing philosophical anthropology by taking the obverse view of (closely inter-related) oppositions between the individual and the collective, or between particular existence and universal human essence, so as to show – as far as possible – *all* the virtualities of simultaneous negation (what I just called the *via negativa*). That is what I would like to do, in an inevitably summary way, in the remainder of this chapter, while keeping in mind three kinds of consideration:

- Firstly, all the philosophers who can be said to have prefigured or initiated a theorisation of the 'transindividual' (or of the human condition as a transindividual condition) at one time or another in their discourse have effected a procedure of *double rejection* of the 'abstractions' that force anthropology to locate the essence of man, be it in the individual, to the detriment of the community (which would then be seen only as the secondary, voluntary or involuntary, contractual or habitual construction of the individual), or be it in social being, to the detriment of the individual (which would then be seen only as the product of the social, more or less completely 'alienable' or detachable from its origin). The logical figure that gives its impetus to their research is therefore a *neither/nor* dealing with contrary terms (individualism versus holism or collectivism), and the resulting problem is to know in what form, within what limits and with what political (or, more generally, practical) function a polarity may be reconstituted.

- Secondly, the very meaning of the discussion and the orientation of the enquiry depend on how the *comparative paradigm* (which I have been led to baptise 'classical') is constructed. In *The Politics of Transindividuality*, Jason Read establishes an originary scene that compares three discourses 'critical' of ontological abstraction: those of Spinoza, Hegel and Marx. All three of these demonstrate that *isolated individuality* (figuring as a 'dominion within a dominion', in Spinoza's famous formula) is an *appearance* produced in the eyes of its bearers themselves by the functioning of the social relation (and this in turn allows this relation to be made to function in the 'subjective' mode of a misunderstanding). I do not disagree with this thesis. If, nevertheless, I substitute Freud for Hegel here (which does not exclude the possibility of re-reading Hegel in light of Freud), it is because I want to show, in all the authors concerned, the presence of a specifically *unconscious* determination, or, if you want, a *double source* for the definition of the social relation. This, in a way, confers a privilege on Freud (without reducing the others' position to his), and cannot be unrelated to the fact that in him the enunciation of the *double rejection* may be the most explicit ('neither psychology nor sociology' allows us to think the phenomena of repression, transference, and identification, as the introduction to *Massenpsychologie und Ich-Analyse* explicitly indicates: this is why we must invent another discipline).[4]

- Thirdly, the concept of *relation* is essentially equivocal in philosophy. Perhaps it is 'said' in as many ways as being itself is: *pollakhôs legomenon*. By a methodological decision, I shall posit that the determination of relations in general as 'social relations' does not reduce this equivocity, but, rather, is itself an example of it. In particular, I shall not decide that one of the protagonists of the virtual debate that I am instituting (so not Marx, but also not Spinoza or Freud either) *possesses the truth* of what the 'social' is. In fact, my working hypothesis is that the social or *social being* must be grounded in the category of the *relation* (which no sociology really does, at least none of those that see in society an original totality, even historically or economically specified), but that there are *several ways of positing the relation* (or of positing that 'there is a relation', of which the 'non-relation' is still a modality) in the modern epoch. This is precisely what the general idea of the 'transindividual' covers, in a programmatically *open* way.

I will now take up the question again point by point, with these hypotheses in mind. I shall begin with Marx, both so that the question of the 'social relation' may be immediately thematised as such, with its contemporary political stakes, and to rectify what has here been incomplete in my previous formulations. I will from there go back to Spinoza, whose intervention in this debate obviously constituted the 'bridge' to an 'ontological' problematic, but also to mark what in him *resists* a universal extension of the schema of transindividuality (I am more conscious of this today than formerly). After all that, I shall delve into Freud, who in my eyes does not represent a 'synthesis' of the previous points of view, but certainly offers the best approach to what they have in common and what distinguishes them.

## Marx and Fetishism: From Alienated Relation to Alienation as Relation

In my previous commentaries, I associated the idea that one finds in Marx the concept of an 'ontology of relations' above all with a re-reading of the statement which appears at the centre of the 1845 *Theses on Feuerbach*: 'But the human essence [das menschliche Wesen] is not an abstraction inherent in the singular individual [kein dem einzelnen Individuum innewohnendes Abstraktum]. In its effective reality [Wirklichkeit] it is the ensemble of social relations [das Ensemble der gesellschaftlichen Verhältnisse]'. Combining suggestions for interpretation from Ernst Bloch with others from Althusser (which may seem daring), I have insisted on the deliberate paradox of this formulation, in which the notion of 'essence' is given an actually 'anti-essentialist' meaning (we can say that this is also the case, by other means, for Spinoza's famous 'definition' of desire: 'desire is the very essence of man', which is to say what *singularises* him as an individual).[5] Above all, I emphasised that, by 'overthrowing' the two Western metaphysical traditions that 'accommodate abstraction' (or the universal) at the heart of individuality (those of Aristotelian naturalism and Augustinian spiritualism), Marx makes the *relation* or the *relationship* (*Verhältnis*) both what 'engenders' or constitutes for each subject its own individuality, lived in a more or less conflictual way, and what makes this individuality immediately 'dependent' on all the other individualities, following the way in which they have been instituted (this generalised 'dependence' can go so far as to be subjugation, or on the contrary can be a practical solidarity opening the way to emancipation).[6] This double constitution is what I have called 'transindividuality' and which, in the ruins of a certain philosophical anthropology, I proposed to consider as a point of departure for an 'ontology of relations' in a materialist sense, so as to mark the irreversibility of the gesture of *double rejection* already mentioned: individuality is not 'autonomous', conceivable separately as a 'first substance' or an 'originary subjectivity'; but neither is it reducible to the totality which encompasses it, whether this is conceived abstractly, as a generic essence, or in an apparently more concrete way, as a society or a community the unity of which is hypostatised.

One could say that transindividuality is, in a sense, axiomatic here. It has a character of immediacy, or of the *given*. It is what is 'originary' (and we will have occasion to revisit the significance of this observation). Two characteristics derive from this: one well known by all the exponents of Marxism, the other less obvious, but to which I have tried to attract attention. Perhaps it is necessary, in reality, to tackle them together. The first, which obviously constitutes the core of Marx's 'critical' intent, is the fact that the 'relational' essence of man has two modes of realisation. In one of these, which one could call the authentic, or 'true' mode, relations of mutual dependence which, for each individual, give a content to their life, are lived and assumed as such, which also confers on the practice of each (whether it be work or cultural) a 'social' dimension of which subjects are the conscious bearers (Marx recalls here the idea of a *generic essence* that he had systematically elaborated in immediately preceding texts).[7] In the other mode, which Marx himself designates as 'alienated' or 'self-alienated' (*[selbst]entfremdet*), individuals are subjects torn from and within themselves (*zerrissen, entzweit*) because they are competing in their very being – which makes them perceive themselves precisely as separate or 'abstract' individualities. Social relations are thus 'desocialised', or separated from their essence, which opens the way to a project of (re) socialisation of the social, which will at the same time be its 'humanisation' (Thesis 10). This does not mean that 'alienated social relations' are no longer social relations, but that they are produced and appear to their bearers (the subjects of 'bourgeois' society) in the form of their opposite (in short, as possessive individualism), which creates for them and for society an unbearable tension, which stokes revolutionary *praxis*. But, on the strongest reading of Marx, this *praxis* is not a subjective choice or a contingent decision; it is nothing other – according to Bloch's excellent expression – than the activation of the 'transformability' or the 'changeability' (*Veränderbarkeit*) inherent to social relations. There is, however, another sense in which one can speak of *Veränderbarkeit*, as I thought I could show by construing the fact that Marx, in the *Theses* (notably in Thesis 6), is careful not to assign to constituent 'social relations' a precise social or institutional *sphere*: it is *indeterminacy* that affects the content and object of social relations, at least in their 'originary' modality, and thus makes them 'plastic' or susceptible to being realised in turn in a multiplicity of 'interactional' situations.[8] These two possible readings are, if not mutually exclusive, at least competing ones in the letter of Marx's text and contribute equally to *posing* the ontological and ethico-political question opened by the name of 'transindividuality'.

It is naturally impossible not to wonder how such a strong intuition is going to develop in Marx's continuation of his work, whether it is labelled 'economic', 'political' or 'philosophical' (distinctions which, we know, are quite irrelevant with regard to his problematic). A whole post-Marxian vein unfolds from the dilemma I have just outlined, by retranslating it in terms of *the division of social labour* and its historical evolution precipitated by capitalism, in order to show that the *return to potential indeterminacy* constitutes the horizon of a revolution of 'productive forces', which would overcome the alienating *specialisation* imposed on individuals by the submission of their activity (and of their life) to capital's logic of valorisation. This is the case for Marx's expansions in (the 1857 manuscript) the *Grundrisse* concerning the emergence of the *general intellect*, and more generally for all the sketches of a definition of 'communism' in the form of a negation of the negation, which led Marx to reaffirm the point of view of the transindividual, not so much in the form of a double rejection (*neither . . . nor . . .*), as in that of an *and . . . and . . .* (or a simultaneous affirmation of opposites): 'communism restores individuality on the basis of the results of capitalist socialisation'.[9] Species being (*Gattungswesen*) is then rethought as a result of the historical development that hypothetically leads capitalism to its negation. I do not deny the importance of this strand in his texts, with the successive enrichment it entails. However, from the *theoretical* perspective that concerns me here, I would like to suggest an alternative, showing that Marx is also conceptually moving in another direction completely, conferring a greater complexity on the idea of the transindividual and contributing to reopening the seemingly resolved anthropological question not by problematising the *alienation of relations* (and, therefore, of the 'social') but, on the contrary, *alienation as a relation* (or, if you like, the alienated relation as a positive concept of the 'society effect').[10] This alternative seems to me essentially to figure in Marx's famous exposition of the 'fetishism of the commodity', on the condition that it is read not just as a denunciation or a warning (which Marx certainly also means it to be), but as the description of a structure that is historically active (in capitalism, and so in the *actuality* of social relations and not in their *origin* or in their hypothetical *end*).

Ideally (but this would inveigle us in an enormous detour), it would be appropriate to grasp the full significance of this proposition to devote the time to putting this in the context of the wake of the Hegelian phenomenology of *intersubjectivity* (and therefore of 'recognition'), as a kind of *counter-phenomenology* in which the question of the scission of the 'subject' between an individual instance (the 'I') and a collective instance (the 'We') and of its reconciliation (*Versöhnung*) in an idea of universal community, instead of being treated exclusively on the side of the subject and its becoming substantial, would be *transposed onto the side of the object* and *of objects*, which is to say onto the field of objectivity, of the 'world of objects' and of their unavoidable role (for example as 'commodities') as intermediaries between subjects. They are the unavoidable *means* and, in fact, determinants of all the relations that 'subjects' or 'men' maintain among themselves. Without being able to develop this argument fully here, I will immediately take up the point of view of the 'interobjectivity' constructed by Marx in his theory of fetishism, and shall try to show how, in relation to the formulations of the *Theses on Feuerbach*, this theory constructs a new notion of the transindividual.[11] I would like to show in particular that the 'society effect' proper to capitalist society, analysed by Marx in this section, which the whole tradition – whether it accepts it or rejects it – concurs in considering a miniature philosophical treatise from which one can interpret the whole 'logic of capital', is actually deployed at *two levels* that are complementary to one another, not as a negation of the negation, but as a kind of redoubled alienation or an alienation within the alienation: the 'fetishism of things' (commodities) and the 'fetishism of persons' (subjects of law). It follows that the transindividual relation does not present itself here as a *simple relation*, which 'relates' individuals to one another, and forms or shapes them through this same relation, but as a *double relation*, with two sides: let us say, for the sake of moving quickly, an economic side and a juridical side, distinct from one another and yet inseparable, like a front and back, but also with an effective 'mediation' of each by the other.[12] Let us briefly explicate these two aspects.

The first consists essentially in the following proposition (taken from the chapter on fetishism):

> the labour of the private individual manifests itself as an element [Glied] of the total labour of society only through the relations which the act of exchange establishes between the products, and, through their mediation, between the producers. To the producers, therefore, the social relations [Beziehungen] between their private labours appear [erscheinen] as what they are, i.e. they do not appear as direct social relations between persons in their work, but rather as material relations between persons and social relations between things [als unmittelbar gesellschaftliche Verhältnisse der Personen in ihren Arbeiten selbst, sondern vielmehr als sachliche Verhältnisse der Personen und gesellschaftliche Verhältnisse der Sachen].[13]

This proposition must be supplemented with everything that the preceding section (devoted to the development of the 'value-form') established: the 'appearance' here, or, better still, the mode of active 'appearing', rests on the fact that commodities, which are immediately objects of material use, *express their exchange value* (representing in the final analysis a certain quantity of labour 'socially necessary' for their production) in the *form of another use value* (which, in developed commodity production, in other words in capitalist production, is always *money*, the 'universal commodity' or 'general equivalent' of all commodities). Not only, therefore, is the *appearance* of commodities as so much exchange value 'expressed' in money not extrinsic to the social relation, but one could say that *without this appearance* or – fictively – 'outside of it' *there is no social relation* between producers and their activities (their 'private labours'). And consequently there are no other social relations (at least in developed capitalist society), for all such relations, in one way or another, pass through the commodity form and money. This is why Marx can write this astonishing phrase: in their alienated form (that of commodity exchange, where individuals 'do not know' one another, except as possessors of commodities and money) social relations appear 'for what they are' (als das, was sie sind). Social relations are not immediate (between the 'members' of society); they are constructed *at a distance*, in the element of commodity exchange and of the value-form, as relations of equivalence between commodities themselves. And there are no other relations. Let us reformulate all of this in terms of transindividuality: we must not fall into the error of calling 'social relations' either a *real* that would be given (or thinkable) independently of their *appearance* (which is to say their form), or an *ideal* situation in which 'personal relations' would also be 'immediately social', without needing to *express themselves* in the form of relations between 'things' (market *equivalence*). Thus it is the system of things exchanged against each other, objectified in monetary expression and more generally that of an *object-value*, 'sensible suprasensible', which not only *makes* individuals *see* the 'society' of which they are members, but also *establishes it*, since without this representation (and its activation in exchange), individual producers *would not exist for one another*, nor would they form 'society'. That this situation may be thought of as alienation, or as the 'inversion' of an ideal, immediately 'personal' relationship, not only does not destroy transindividuality, but constitutes it.

All this is well enough known to readers of Marx (although they sometimes interpret it in a different terminology), but in my opinion it constitutes only the first half of his construction. His exposition of 'commodity fetishism' certainly aims to demonstrate that the necessary illusion thus named is constitutive of *economic objectivity*: provocatively fusing what a good Kantian philosopher, using the same categories, would have distinguished as an 'analytic' of objective knowledge and a 'dialectic' of ideology, it installs at the heart of objectivity, as a condition of the possibility of experience, a fundamental 'misunderstanding'. This is summarised in the formula: their own social relations (starting with the social division of labour) appear to individuals ('producer-exchangers') as relations (of value) between things (which is to say commodities). But this demonstration of 'economic' forms must be supplemented by a symmetrical demonstration that focuses on the 'fetishism of persons', in other words, the equally necessary illusion that is implied in the juridical and moral notion of the 'person'. This counterpart is more difficult for the traditional commentary to grasp, on the one hand because it figures in a separate discussion,[14] and on the other because it forces us to resolve a dilemma concerning the notion of the 'person' that in fact goes well beyond a question of terminology. Marx speaks of *Personen*, sometimes to designate *human individuals in general*, qua natural or quasi-natural 'bearers' (*Träger*) of social relations (analogous in this sense to 'use-values' which bear the value of commodities), and sometimes to designate the *juridical form* (analogous to the 'value-form' of exchange value) under which they mutually perceive each other as subjects, and enter into a process of recognition. In short, it is a matter of breaking through the enigma of the 'personal' appearance of persons themselves. The reason for this supplement is in fact indicated even within the preceding discussion, when Marx explains that the *effect of social objectivity* borne by commodities qua 'double' objects does not result from a simple passive 'perception' (in this sense, the vocabulary of *appearance* is misleading, at least if one construes it in the traditional cognitive sense), but from a *practice*, that of exchange (which is based on the 'market'). Indeed, commodities 'cannot take themselves to market': they must be *brought* there to be *exchanged* there for one another (and in fact always through the intermediary of money held by the exchangers). Having shown that social relations present themselves as relations between things, Marx must now show that relations between things do not exist without the intervention or mediation of 'persons', which are linked together by a different social relation, or by a different aspect of the preceding one.

As we know from having read or re-read Chapter 2 of Book I, this relation is constructed around the 'abstract' categories (which is to say, categories which are universal and adaptable to any concrete situation and to any particular individuality) of ownership and contract, the system of which is like a mirror image of the 'economic' relations of appropriation and equivalence.[15] The equivalence of commodities thus corresponds to the *legal equality* required between the partners of a contract of sale and purchase, whatever it may be (formal equality, or the equality 'of rights'). And this in turn is possible only through the *freedom* of the contractors, which means, negatively, that they are not in relationships of dependence or servitude among themselves, and, positively, that they are all deemed *proprietors*, specifically 'proprietors of their own person', to quote Locke's seminal formulation. At this level, an *intersubjectivity*, or rather, an (institutional) *effect* of intersubjectivity, constructed by means of the law, therefore reappears, with which subjects identify so to be able to play their role (*Charactermaske*) in the setting up and practical implementation of *their own* 'economic' *social relations*. This is how Marx can write: 'the characters who appear on the economic stage are merely [juridical] personifications of economic relations; it is as the bearers of these economic relations that they come into contact with each other'.[16] Economic agents (capitalists, wage-workers, merchants, etc.) never meet (*gegenübertreten*) in the original nakedness of simply 'living' human beings. They can meet usefully, which is to say socially, only if they have (in advance) become autonomous, individualised persons, recognised as such, and if, therefore, they cannot be confused with 'things'. In Marx's problematic, this means that the juridical forms which liberate the individual for exchange (and, where applicable, for exploitation) constitute a *second level of alienation*, at one and the same time original and correlative to the preceding one, into which it is in practice inserted to ensure its realisation. The economic *informs* the juridical and the juridical *activates* the economic.

It is this complex form, precisely this *double structuring*, at once reciprocal and dissymmetrical, that I propose to consider the new, developed concept of the 'transindividual' in Marx's theory. From the ideas sketched from the sixth 'Thesis on Feuerbach' onwards, his theory incontestably maintains this central philosophical intuition: the double rejection of individualist and holistic (organicist) ontologies and their socio-political consequences, in favour of giving primacy to the relation, or to a constituent relation. But his theory undergoes a conversion in relation to the idea that there is an 'authenticity' of relations that, in a certain way, had been lost through their alienated historical forms. It is these alienated forms that are henceforth (in association with a certain historical anthropology) contrariwise responsible for constructing the transindividual or, as I have suggested in Althusser's words, for producing the 'society effect' for individuals themselves. I am not ignoring, of course, the fact that this view of things must raise, for every reader of Marx, a series of problems, even difficulties. On the one hand, it seems uncertain that this understanding of the transindividual applies, not only in 'non-market' or 'non-capitalist' societies where double alienation is not present (or does not play the same universally structuring role), but especially in the hypothetical *communism*, to which, across his work, Marx always refers to explicate the difference between a directly 'social' organisation of production and an 'indirect', 'unconscious' organisation of the expenditure of social labour (through the intermediary of the market), thus, last but not least, to explain that this could one day historically disappear. In what sense could communism be thought in the register of transindividuality, and even as a modality of 'social relations', if it is to coincide structurally with the double alienation described above? It seems (and I will come back to this) that the idea of communism now represents not an achievement of the idea of the transindividual, but an *exception* or even a *vanishing point* in relation to its logic. On the other hand, does rethinking, in terms of alienation, the very relation that makes up the reality or the effectivity of the social not take too lightly Marx's insistence on the 'phantasmagoric' character of social forms designated by the name of fetishism (itself immediately associated with notions of 'delirium', 'confusion' or hallucination)? I will say not – indeed, to the contrary – but only on condition that all these terms, which push the idea of an *objective imaginary* inherent in social relations to the extreme, are precisely what makes it possible to understand (beyond a problematic of transcendental illusion with which, however, they have an undeniable affinity) in what sense the transindividual must present itself to individuals in an inverted form (not as what constitutes them structurally into subjects, but as what they could decide to institute or not to institute). Or even, as Jason Read rightly insists here, the structure explains in what sense 'social relations' are manifested in the form of a relation between autonomous individuals.[17] Social reality must take on a hallucinatory character, or be woven from fantasy, in order to exist as such, in history and in practice. It is at this point that, without a doubt, the 'detour via Spinoza' can become illuminating again.

## Spinoza and the Double Constitution of the City

In Spinoza too, although his position is at first sight very different and draws on entirely other philosophical sources, the 'interhuman' relation is thought as a double relation, or as *presenting a double aspect*. He made this discovery at a time when he thought the human condition to be intrinsically *political* (or that politics is the immediate form of *ethics*). This idea runs through all his works, especially the two 'treatises' (*Political* and *Theological*

*Political*), but it is systematised and demonstrated in Part IV of the *Ethics* (significantly entitled 'On Human Bondage', which is not far removed from the idea of alienation, particularly if one reads in the term 'bondage' the idea of subjection, or of a condition of dependence which we have not chosen). And it is on this basis that his philosophy has been presented by different authors (including myself) as a philosophy in which 'metaphysics' and 'politics' are coextensive. I would like now to return to this point by focusing both on striking analogies between his approach and that of Marx (particularly regarding thinking the social relation as a 'double relation') and on what distinguishes them (in particular, their very different conception of the functions of the imaginary in human practice).

I shall begin with a difficulty which appeared to me in re-reading the remarks I had previously devoted to the discussions in Part IV of the *Ethics* in which Spinoza arrives at his notion of the 'double genesis' of the city, by combining the analyses he devoted respectively to the *imitation of affects*, as a process which makes individuals' complexes of ideas and desires circulate amongst them, and to the *common notions* that rational minds forge by thinking everything together as parts of nature. I have twice in succession found myself revisiting the 'demonstrative complex' built around Proposition 37 of Part IV ('The good which everyone who seeks virtue wants for himself, he also desires for other men; and this desire is greater as his knowledge of God is greater'): in Chapter 4 of my short book *Spinoza and Politics*, and in my Rijnsburg lecture (Chapter 1 of the present volume), but according to two different modalities.

In *Spinoza and Politics*, I took up the point of view of an anthropology in the Spinozist sense, which is to say, of a chain of consequences which follow from the definition of 'man's very essence' as *desire* (*cupiditas*). I showed that, if man's essence always pertains to his individual singularity, this, in reality, cannot be isolated from a network of relations with other individuals that *determines* it, and in which this essence is always simultaneously active and passive, affected by others and affecting others. But this reciprocity can itself be read according to two modalities, each of which Spinoza analytically correlates to one of the two competing 'demonstrations' he proposes for Proposition 37: the modality of passionate exchanges for which the motor is the ambivalent (and unstable) desire (*flutuatio animi*) of each person to identify themselves with others and that of others to identify themselves with that person (*ambitio*); and the modality of rational calculation that leads each person to understand that their own utility resides in the existence of a society where the forces of all, instead of neutralising or destroying each other, compose a superior power to act (and to preserve everyone). Taken together, these two components of Spinoza's reasoning combine to show that 'social human nature' is a compound, in variable proportions, not of the mind and the body, but of dispositions and actions that 'obey reason' and others that 'proceed from passion'. The upshot of this is that the affective composition of singular individuality and the conjunction, in the institution of the city, of rational 'forces' and passionate forces are simply the front and reverse sides of the same question, because individual dispositions themselves have a *relational* essence, whether this follows the modality of imitation or that of utility. They are both causes and effects of the 'social' relation in which each individual finds themselves always already with everyone else, and therefore these effects *express* it.[18] In other words, the Spinozist argument, founded on an astonishing 'parallelism' of the first two 'kinds of knowledge', which would seem first of all to have no object other than showing that it is possible to explain and justify the existence of social institutions, *as much* from the point of view of the imagination as from that of reason (which also allows the 'phenomenological' clarification of different aspects of *sociability*), finally proves to be a *practical refutation* of the idea that one could *segregate*, as two objects of study and two distinct realities, human individuality from society. This reversibility does *not negate* the possibility of 'defining' them as two correlative points of view, but does not permit them to be *abstracted* from one another. It is the very object of philosophical *anthropology*, on which it confers from the outset a political character (from which it is possible to draw conclusions about the vicissitudes of the life of the state). I did not use the category of the 'transindividual' in this book, but I posited that the whole philosophy of Spinoza has no other objective, at base, than that of constructing and comparing *modes of communication*, which sometimes operate at the level of affects, and sometimes at the level of rational ideas.

In my talk at Rijnsburg, by contrast, I tried to construct the *ontology of the transindividual* that this anthropology appears to illustrate while constituting its implicit objective. I will not repeat this whole argument, which I have not resiled, here, even if certain aspects of it seem problematic to me, but I shall recapitulate its guiding thread: the primacy of *individuation* (the formation, preservation and variation of individual forms), and above all the impossibility of separating *individuation* from *individualisation* (that is, the question of knowing what capacity an individual possesses, by virtue of their own power, to *determine themselves*), since both depend on the *conatus* or the 'power to act' of singular beings. I argued that, for Spinoza, every individual in nature is in reality a 'transindividual', which is to say a 'finite' relational mode. This leads to a paradoxical ontology, in which individuals conserve themselves by virtually *decomposing* and *recomposing* themselves, constantly 'exchanging' with other individuals 'parts' or 'affections' that they share with them as a function of the larger and more complex 'totality' into which they must integrate to survive (for example a 'city'). Three levels of existence, or of horizontal and vertical relations, therefore intervene here to ensure that the 'individual' remains relatively stable by virtue of its own *conatus*, resisting decomposition more or less effectively.[19] The advantage of this way of putting things, it seems to me, is that it goes beyond a merely *critical* understanding of the double rejection of individualism and holism, in favour of a *constructive* interpretation in which this double rejection is only the counterpart of the invention of a structure of expression and development of *activities* (I agree with Deleuze here), because everything that 'is', to 'act and operate' (as Spinoza says), must also permanently be able to *be affected* and thus *altered* in its very being. This is the definition of the *conatus*, the true object of Spinozist ontology.[20]

We must, then, conclude, with Jason Read in particular, that isolated individuality is a mere semblance, as well as an alienated modality (Spinoza would call it inadequate or impotent), the cause of which must be sought in the weakness of the transindividual, but on condition that we add immediately the opposite semblance, that of a self-sufficient totality deriving its power to exist from its pure collective 'form' (or, in more political terms, from its 'regime'), is equally inadequate. Now, this point leads immediately to a difficulty from an 'ontological' perspective, of which I have not been sufficiently cognisant: it clings to the *analogical use* of the concept of the individual (and therefore also of the 'transindividual', or of transindividual individuation) to which it is still captive. This results in a tendency to *substitute* the ontological argument thus reformulated for the phenomenology of 'passionate' and 'rational' forms of sociability, and thus *either* to relativise their opposition (by making their 'expressions' more or less adequate to the same *conatus*) *or* to make one of them the *truth* of the other, by imagining a teleological process of transformation from one to the other. All these orientations constitute, in fact, simplifications of what Spinoza sought to highlight with his notion of an anthropological 'double genesis' of sociability. They make it more difficult to understand how the relation between the philosophy of the *Ethics* and the 'concrete' analyses of the two political *Treatises* (in which what comes to the fore is precisely the sharpness of the tension between the passionate and the rational) is established. And, above all, they contradict a philological fact of which – in seeking to draw lessons from others' attempts at interpretation – I have since sought to show the full import: when Spinoza comes to describe the effects of integration and consensus (or unanimity) which make the 'political body' exist and confer on it a capacity to form common ideas, he does not speak of a simple superior *individuality*, but of a *quasi-individuality*. This obviously does not mean that we should fall back on an 'individualist' conception (and in particular not on a contractarian one) of the formation of political bodies, but that we must abandon the *anthropomorphic* analogy (found especially in Hobbes) and conceive their conservation (and also their dissolution) *on a different model* to that of particular human individualities. That this refutation of the analogy leads in the end not to renouncing the notion of the 'transindividual', but on the contrary to enriching it, is what I would now like to show, beginning with a brief review of the meaning of the *quasi-individuality* of cities or political units.[21]

The formula identifying the 'right of the state' with the 'potentia multitudinis, quae una veluti mente ducitur' – the power of the multitude which is expressed when it is directed *as if by a single mind* (or, following an alternative translation: when it can be considered as being directed by a single mind) – appears in the *Political Treatise* in Section 2 of Chapter 3. One finds repetitions and partial equivalents at other points in his work, notably in the *Ethics*, where, in a highly significant way, Spinoza reconstructs the correlation of the modalities of our collective existence under the two attributes of body and thought:

> To man, then, there is nothing more useful than man. Man, I say, can wish for nothing more helpful to the preservation of his being than that all should so agree in all things [omnes in omnibus ita convenient] that the minds and bodies of all would compose, as it were, one mind and one body [ut omnium Mentes and Corpora unam quasi Mentem, unumque Corpus component].[22]

What is important here is that the analogy of 'forms of individuality' emerging at different levels is indeed taken up as a thread, but this analogy is immediately relativised, or, rather, modalised. What does this modal difference consist in? I think that it essentially consists in this: that the 'composite' that is a singular human individual (often referred to in the *Ethics* by the simple name *unusquisque*)[23] and the 'composite' that is the social body endowed with a particular political 'constitution', made up of multiple institutions, do not have the same degree of *stability*. This, in turn, is due to the fact that the *conflicts* likely to make it decompose are uneven in intensity and do not all obey the same logic. In the body politic, not only are these not neutralised or suppressed by a 'normal' health regime, but, rather, are recurrent, and even constitute (as is explained in Chapter 17 of the

*Theological Political Treatise* based on Machiavelli and Tacitus) the principal danger for its survival, being far more formidable than external dangers (or, if you will, it is by dint of forces of internal disintegration that external dangers become more or less serious).[24] To this contention, however, another must immediately be juxtaposed pushing us in the opposite direction: as Spinoza's constant thesis is that human individuals can survive, preserve themselves, cultivate themselves, and develop their 'power to act' only insofar as they pool common resources incorporated in the city (which is really a *utility*), the greater stability from which they benefit and which makes it possible to speak of a relatively *autonomous* individuality itself has the stability of the city as a condition, such that if the city only has an ephemeral existence or finds itself permanently exposed to disorders and civil wars, human beings themselves will only have a precarious existence. This is why it is of *vital* interest to human individuals to preserve and improve the constitution of their city, even while they are competing with one another and in conflict inside it.

Hence the necessity for us to finish by shifting up to a third kind of consideration: in the case of collective (social or political) individuality, what determines the identity of the composite is first of all the degree and mode of composition of minds, whereas in the case of singular individuality, it is first of all the mode of composition of the body. Despite the formal doctrine of the equality of the attributes of substance, an inversion occurs which reflects a different relationship between existence, consciousness and intelligibility. Spinoza explains that an individual's mind (*mens*) is a set of (partly clear, partly confused) ideas whose common material referent is the human body with its affections, whereas what makes it possible to speak of a 'body politic' is the fact that the mass of the citizens reach sufficient *unanimity* that their bodies and the corresponding powers of action are 'conducted' sustainably in the same direction.[25] Absolute unanimity, however, is impossible, or, rather, it is a contradiction in terms, because it supposes the dissolution of the very 'characters' (*ingenia*) that constitute it and which push individuals to express themselves in a heterogeneous way, following their own *conatus* and the singularity of their desire. This is why collective or social individuality is only approximate or even inadequate (as indicated by the prepositions *quasi* and *veluti*). From another point of view, however, this inadequacy is a greater complexity, and thus virtually a greater power. What I have said implies that, rather than a negative or defective ontological characteristic, it is a permanent *political problem*. The bodies politic of which Spinoza speaks (even when they seem to have acquired very great power) are those complex individualities whose very possibility is for their components an everyday question to be resolved and something at stake in their *praxis*.

In conclusion, I think that we can rethink the question of the *transindividual as a double relation* together with the ontological dimension of what was, first of all, a problematic of political anthropology. I will propose to do this by combining three notions: that of the *ratio* (even of the 'correct ratio') that must obtain between the forms of passionate sociability and the rational ones in order for a city to be preserved, for a certain time at least (and consequently to ensure the survival and intellectual progress of its 'citizens'); that of the *reciprocal presupposition* (in the form of a 'chiasm') which ties together the registers of the imaginary and reason (as genres of knowledge, forms of life and modes of communication) to produce 'the society effect'; and lastly, that of the *transition* or tendential *transformation* by which one can say that this composite is always affected, although within determinate limits (one could say, within a certain 'finitude'), and under the regime of ontological *fragility*. Because Spinoza never ceases to aim at stability, but what he theorises is at base the precariousness that life must overcome.

The grouping constituted around Proposition 37 of Part IV has a strange tension within it. On the one hand, it suggests a possibility of substituting what I have called the two 'geneses' of sociability, that which 'passes' through 'mimetic' mechanisms of the imagination by which individuals affect one another, and that which 'passes' through the 'calculus' (in the sense of the anticipation of the consequences of certain causes) of the utility which results from *convenientia*, for one another.[26] Everything happens as if 'passionate' sociability and 'rational' sociability, the logic of imitation and the logic of utility, constitute the two terms of an epistemological *dilemma*. But, on the other hand, in accordance with the general direction of Part IV, it suggests that the objective of common utility corresponds to a recognition of the primacy of reason over passion and the affective instability it implies. These are, then, virtually at least, the two moments of a *progression*. How should we interpret this tension? Should it be minimised, or, on the contrary, assigned a decisive significance? It is striking to observe that, in recent commentary, contrary to the rationalist tendencies that had previously prevailed among Spinoza's readers (even in the case of Alexandre Matheron), his interpreters have been more and more inclined not only to emphasise the function of the imagination, but to *restore the imagination* as the principle of sociability, precisely because of the 'transindividual' nature of affective life, the dynamic of which it expresses in ideas.[27] I think that, as always with Spinoza, we must get out of this dilemma by rectifying the image of a parallelism in favour of that of a *ratio*: all cities are constituted – which is to say, 'unified' – *at one and the same time* through passionate mechanisms and rational expedience. The former oscillate in an unpredictable way between love and hatred, antithetical but also capable of 'cementing' communities, and the latter are more or less conscious, or publicly recognised, which allows them to act *after the fact* on the former with more or less efficacy. The ratio is therefore never determined once and for all, but engaged in a process of transformation or 'transition' within its own structure.[28]

Does this, for all that, imply a teleology or a doctrine of the historical progress of reason? Not exactly, it seems to me, even if there is a striking *bias* in favour of reason, for two closely interrelated reasons, which can be said to express Spinoza's ontology of his conception of the 'finite modes of substance' even within his political anthropology. The first is that the transition does have a causal necessity, but no predetermined orientation, and, *a fortiori*, is not irreversible. It *can* be oriented towards a maximal power of the multitude, guaranteeing at the same time, by means of determinate institutions, the greatest autonomy of individuals (in particular from the point of view of freedom of thought), which corresponds for Spinoza to the *democratic tendency* immanent in all political regimes. But it *can also* be reversed into a decomposition, even a self-destruction of society. Perhaps, following a 'pessimism' inherited from Machiavelli, this reversal is inevitable, even though it cannot be foreseen, and even though, through the exercise of civic *virtue*, one may even be able to delay it.[29] The second reason, underlying the first, is that imagination and reason form, in the political field, a circle of reciprocal presupposition, or, better still, a *chiasm*. Theoretically, this is the crucial point. The idea of a city entirely constituted by imaginary mechanisms (logics of passionate *imitation*, of a religious, national, or more generally ideological type) is absurd: there must be a rational utility that is not only 'immanent' in the manner of an *invisible hand*, but *recognised* by the citizens, which is the function of *institutions*, the forms and subjective effects of which Spinoza studies in his two *Treatises*, to be able to act on them from within. But the idea of a *rational city*, without an affective and imaginary 'base', so without an idea of 'good' and 'evil', of the 'just' and 'unjust', an economy of hope and fear, is just as devoid of signification. I believe that this thesis is implicit in the very way in which Spinoza uses the strategic category of the 'similar' to define the 'common good' as a model of life 'according to the guidance of reason'. The similar one, for each man, is 'the other man', thus, conversely, he is the model of his own humanity (the religious tradition calls him 'his neighbour'). In order that citizens may establish among themselves the bonds of reciprocal convenience for which Spinoza has reserved the name of *friendship*, and which he sees as the source of a stable joy, and thereby of communal power or liberty, the other people must appear to him, precisely, as similar, and therefore be *presented* to him *by the imagination*.[30] The chiasm therefore consists in the fact that there is an instance of reason operating within the play of passions, so as to orient it towards a constructive power (what Negri would call a 'constituent power'), and even so that there is an instance of the imagination that operates in the order of common notions, so as to furnish them with an 'object' or 'material'. This double instance is the city or society itself, in its constitutive instability.[31]

## Freud and the *Massenbildungen*: Identification and Institution

Here, then, we arrive at the final station on our journey: Freud, in his turn read, or re-read, in the light of a comparison with the theories of the transindividual relation that I have identified in Marx and Spinoza. Within Freud's oeuvre, I am restricting my focus to his book, published in 1921, *Mass Psychology and the Analysis of the Ego*, because its theory of the correlation between the formation of the 'ego' (*Ich* – which in English actually means 'I') and that of the 'groups' or 'masses' constitutes *the* key moment in overcoming the opposition between 'individual' and 'collective' psychology. This is what I propose to call the *moment of the transindividual* in Freud's oeuvre. The other reason why I have privileged this text is that it is one of those that truly mark a turning point in the history of political philosophy, outside of which in particular the politico-theoretical configuration of the European twentieth century remains unintelligible.[32] Naturally, these two points are not independent: there is a relationship of reciprocal presupposition between them. With others, I have argued that, if the introduction of the unconscious[33] radically transforms our understanding of the political field, the opposite is no less true: its conjunction with politics does not proceed without tension or contradictions, but this is *implied* by the definition of the unconscious, insofar as this, precisely, is not reducible either to individual psychology or to social psychology.

I will first observe that Freud's whole text is marked by inversions and reversibility. There exists a profound solidarity between these different operations, which bear on the foundational categorical antitheses of philosophy, politics and the *episteme* underlying the 'human sciences'. This is the case for the antitheses of the individual and the collective (or the social), on the one hand, and for the normal and the pathological, on the other. One notes from the opening of Freud's text a cautious but clear stand against the idea of opposing an *Individualpsychologie* to a *Sozial- oder Massenpsychologie*. This opposition, according to Freud, must be surpassed (and obviously it is up to psychoanalysis to provide the means for this). The rest of the book shows that there are basically two ways of understanding this. There is what I will call a *weak* way, which consists in showing the complementarity of the phenomena of individual psychology and of collective psychology without modifying their definitions. It is rational to study them together, within the frame of the same science. But beyond this there is a logically *strong* way, which consists in demonstrating, through the theoretical construction of 'unconscious desire', that the individual and the collective belong to a single *structure*, of which they constitute functions that are themselves reversible. This is the point of view that the text will progressively elaborate, the culmination of which is constituted (in Chapter 8, 'Being in Love and Hypnosis') by the drawing and interpretation of the graph of identification,[34] inasmuch as it can be read in either direction, *either* from the division of the subject into the *Ich* (ego) and the *Ichideal* (ego ideal) towards the substitution of one and the same 'external object' for the objects on which the libido in the amorous state is fixed, and therefore towards that X, whatever it may be, which the subjects have 'in common' and which renders them indistinct, *or*, conversely, from the libidinal indistinction (the common *object* which renders them interchangeable, not to say indiscernible) *towards* the division which it induces in the subject (*ego* against *ego ideal*, 'what in me is worth more than me').[35] In introducing the provocative idea that love and hypnosis constitute 'mass formations of two' (*Massenbildungen zu zweit*), and that hypnosis, in particular, is not simply external in relation to the social and political 'mass' because in reality they have the same structure, Freud is preparing an even more radical reversal, which will be accomplished in the final chapter, ironically entitled 'Postscript': it will consist in presenting individualisation itself as a *particular case* of *Massenbildung* or mass formation (inasmuch of course as this is a 'formation of the unconscious').

His typology follows an apparently arithmetic criterion:[36] the 'mass of many' (*zu vielen*, which is to say formally more than three) is the institutional mass, composed or in the process of decomposition. Then there are the 'masses of two' (*Masse zu zweit*), which have antithetical principles: on the one hand, the amorous relationship; and on the other, the hypnotic relationship. The dissociation of these two makes it possible to interpret the presence, in the functioning of institutions as well as in the circumstances of individual existence, of two great principles corresponding at least indirectly to an intrinsic duality of the identificatory model: on the one hand (this is the lineage of 'love') there is what Freud calls *the overvaluation of the object* (or the denial of its defects); on the other (the lineage of 'hypnosis') the *suspension of the judgement of reality*, or, better, the 'delegation' to the other of *the testing of reality*, which the subject renounces for himself in installing truth in the other (who can be a leader, a teacher, even a professor or an ideology).

And finally, which is obviously the most remarkable thing, there is what Freud calls the 'mass of one' (*Masse zu eins, Einsamkeit*), which is to say the isolated individual as an intrinsically fragile, aleatory effect of a certain negative modality (or privation) of the previous relations which 'isolates' from others those who bear them, rendering identification impossible, or at least painful and difficult for them. This idea is stated right at the beginning of the text, and it reappears at the end in a way that is at this point 'well founded', but also in an extremely significant variant, which can also be considered an indicator of a difficulty within the Freudian elaboration. Because of this *isolation*, which is itself a relational phenomenon, and a function of the 'mass', Freud needs experimental, even generalising models that bring out its lived modality. The introduction of the book cites Bleuler's autism, albeit with caution, whereas the conclusion refers to a neurosis which is at base our common condition. But these are really not the same thing! An 'autistic' model suggests that the relation of the individuality to the mass, by the intermediary of the affective relation, is essentially *negative* or even *destructive*. Describing a wrenching away from language, it mandates a return to an opposition between the 'normal' and the 'pathological', and either that the pole of the pathological be assigned to the individual, or, in a projective fashion, it be assigned to society or to the institution of which the individual is the victim. But it has the non-negligible advantage of suggestion that *extreme violence* is an immanent possibility of processes of individualisation, inasmuch as they are themselves modes of 'socialisation', just as it is the immanent possibility of the process of aggregation or of 'massification'. By contrast, a 'neurotic' model suggests, not exactly a *positivity* of being in an individualised relation, but an essential *ambivalence* or 'uncertainty', affective as well as representative: what one can call a 'subject's ill-being', correlative to the 'malaise of civilisation' that affects its very constitution.

Throughout the book, the primacy and even the autonomy of 'individual psychology' have been negated, not in favour of a primacy of the social or the sociological but in favour of their equivalence, as being dependent on the same structure: let us say that of the transindividual.[37] This structure is the *ensemble* of four 'mass formations', or is itself the 'mass' qua complex of four 'formations': the institutional mass, the isolated or 'neurotic' individual who finds their place in society, and the two transferential forms, antithetical to one another (but reunited in the formation of institutions) of the hypnotic relation and the amorous relation. Precisely because it is neither individualistic nor holistic, the Freudian schema is symmetrically open to the dual question of *modalities of totalisation* and *modalities of individualisation* (rather than *of individuation*, since we are here on the plane of the psychological conditions of people's social autonomy). These two symmetrical questions are inscribed in a typology of the effects of the structure, which is a typology of the variants of *being in relation*, as psychoanalysis allows us to interpret them.

Here we see the possibility of 'defining' or 'characterising' psychoanalysis, as a science, precisely through this doubly critical operation that has a thoroughly political meaning. But first we must combine the effects of this with those of a second, even more obviously 'political', reversal, one which affects the categories of the normal and the pathological. This point is in principle difficult because, throughout his work, Freud never ceased to oscillate between different possible positions, ranging from the resumption of the founding postulate of positivist medicine according to which the pathological is a deviation from the normal, to the idea that the 'normal' is a pathological case that ignores itself, or to the idea that psychoanalysis suspends all distinction between these 'values'.[38] But in the *Massenpsychologie* a radical operation is carried out against both common representations and the 'theoretical' elaboration proposed by Le Bon in his 1895 *La psychologie des foules* (which was translated into

German in 1912), from whom Freud borrows a whole phenomenology, but the direction of which he completely reverses. Le Bon and the theorists of crowd psychology in general privileged the example of the revolutionary movements characterised by the belief of those who adhere to them in the 'omnipotence of ideas'. For these theorists, the constitution of these crowds is a pathological phenomenon *par excellence*. It defines a disease of the political order, against which state and society must defend themselves. For Freud, on the contrary, the affective and cognitive processes which degrade the capacity of the subject to judge autonomously and destroy the rationality of the collective apply *first to the institutions of the established order*, of which he takes as examples the Church and the army. These are the true 'primary crowds' and we might hear here an intra-psychoanalytic play on words: in order to witness the emergence of a 'primary process', there is no need to examine social and political phenomena that are considered pathological, as well as criminal, by the dominant rationality; it suffices to observe the cohesion of institutions and the adhesion they command.[39] Or, more precisely, these institutions should be considered as *defence mechanisms* against the phenomena of disintegration which always threaten them from within, towards which they must constantly mobilise the powers of thought and of unconscious affectivity, which are, nevertheless, fundamentally of the same nature. In Chapter 5 of the book, Freud identifies these phenomena very precisely: for the army, he cites panic or disorder; and for the Church, sectarianism and intolerance. Thus, the army figures as that organisation woven from libido which resists panic (unless it yields to it), just as the Church appears as that organisation which resists intolerance (unless it yields to it). This inversion deconstructs the ideologemes of order and disorder, and introduces into the heart of politics a fundamentally *impolitic* dimension, beyond which the very concept of politics is empty. Politics is a violence which turns against itself, and thus assumes the form of order and cohesion.[40] But it is equally crucial psychologically because it is the unconscious matrix or game of representations and affects that 'fixes' individuals in a collective conformism, or, on the contrary, propels them into the uncontrollable element of a subversive or self-destructive 'disconnect'.

Between the two points that we have just mentioned, there is, moreover, again a close connection, since judgements of normality are conditioned by the maintenance of a *distance* between the individual personality and its incorporation in mass movements, and conversely institutions and social situations are judged normal or pathological depending on whether they favour or abolish the distance between the individual and the collective. The opposition between these two poles of psychology is a necessary fiction which is maintained by a social order that rests, in the final analysis, on their indistinction. It is, obviously, at the level of these interpretations of the functioning of the great state apparatuses, the army and the Church, that the indistinction of the political register and the psychoanalytic register appears most immediately. I have spoken of examples, but this qualification ought now to be revisited. The army and the Church cannot be mere *examples*, because their 'artificial' (*künstlich*) character, paradoxically combined with a 'high degree of organisation' and of stability, rests, according to Freud, both on an 'external constraint' (*äusserer Zwang*) and on a 'libidinal linking structure' (*libidinöse Struktur, Libidobindungen*). It is therefore also based on the overdetermined combination of an involuntary adherence with a deliberate adhesion, which can only come from a long history. Placing this discussion in the context of the dissolution of the Austro-Hungarian Empire as a result of war and its own internal social tensions,[41] it is difficult not to suppose that this combination is meant to describe the two 'pillars' of the state, or of a certain authoritarian type of state. In other words, it names the state metonymically.[42]

The last remarkable characteristic of the institutions compared by Freud concerns the *double modality* of the identifications that his extensive use of the word 'leader' (*Führer*) covers. In the case (and the type) of the army, the leader is 'real', or, rather, he is living, visible, even if the libidinal investment of which he is the object is phantasmatic, and this living reality, which one is tempted to call an incarnation, equally colours the proofs of love that members of the military crowd expect of him, together and separately. In the case (and the type) of the (Catholic) Church, the true – which is to say mystical – 'leader', who is not the Pope but Christ, is an 'idea', that is to say, he is someone dead represented as the bearer of the very life of the living, and this characteristic also colours the phantasmatic modality of the libidinal connection, which implies a sublimation or a desexualisation. In the end, what appears above all is the intrinsic division of the idea of an 'object' or a 'model' (*Vorbild*) of identifications. If therefore one speaks not of just *some* contingent and multiple identifications which are identifiable at difference scales and in different contexts, but about identification in the *singular*, as a structure or mechanism constitutive of social life, which has the constitution of the individual 'ego', both autonomous and interdependent, as its correlate, we see that identification requires both these two modalities, 'real' and 'ideal', inscribed in the field of the unconscious. It is their complementarity which gives efficacy to the connection to which Freud gives the generic name of 'mass'. But at the same time, Freud's exposition seems to include astonishing elisions. One of them concerns the fact that crowds, or some of them, are not only based on a pooling of libidinal investment, but are actually gendered, constructed on an internal or external use of the difference between the sexes. Freud is surprisingly elusive on this point, which also confers the character of a denial to the way he exposes the constitutive homosexuality of political institutions, which he describes without ever naming it as such. Likewise, he is elusive about the fact that the very identifications of which he speaks are not only identifications with a positive model, but also negative identifications by rejection and exclusion of the enemy or foreign body, in other words, via hate and not only love (a point that Spinoza on the other hand systematically emphasises).[43]

I can then return to my idea of a specifically Freudian elaboration of *the ontology of relations*. I have said several times that if Freud's point of view is not 'individualist', it is not 'holistic' either. He postulates no pre-existence, no pre-eminence of 'the whole' in relation to individuals or parts. We can even suppose that it is the threat of the dissolution of 'the whole', thus its intrinsic fragility, that needs to be averted by a reiterated identification. It is from this that the phantasmagorical representation of *the exclusion of the foreign body* proceeds as the operation that consists in making the *social* or *political body* exist as a supposedly given 'totality', be it a people, a race or a fraternity. The elements which thus produce an effect of totalisation, however, are not directly 'individuals', but – as in Spinoza – the *affects of individuals*, linked to 'representations' of what makes them similar and dissimilar. In other words, these are *relations of individuals* in the imaginary, which are given *at the same time as them*, or are one with them, even if they divide them as much as they unite them. Freud is here again astonishingly close to Spinoza, and to a lesser degree to Marx: the society he tells us about is not a formation of individuals, but a *formation of relations*. And for that to be the case – this is the very meaning of the graph at the end of Chapter 8 – relations must be combined together according to the scheme of a double *mimesis*, functioning simultaneously horizontally between 'similar things', and vertically, as an identification with a 'model' (*Vorbild*), itself equally imaginary, the power of attraction and suggestion of which induces, by a recursive effect, the *Spaltung* or splitting of the subject. All this was, in a certain way, given in embryo in the relational matrix that Freud, 'punctuating' his own exposition of an *afterthought*, exposes in the modality of this double unity of opposites exhibited by the tableau of the *Massenbildungen*.

## The Transindividual, a Quasi-transcendental?

Obviously, I cannot definitively conclude such a comparative discussion (which in any case covers here only some of the authors or works that should be invoked, in particular the analyses proposed by Jason Read and in the collective anthologies cited above). And I would never want to give the impression that there is a 'philosophy of the transindividual' of which Marx, Spinoza and Freud's doctrines would give us a kind of illustration. I would, rather, try to open up discussion around themes that have a more general scope for anthropology. At the same time as I approach these, I am seeking the best terminology to define them.

To begin with, I would like to bring to the fore a precisely 'ontological' consideration that came to my attention only because I was re-reading Spinoza with the analogies and the oppositions between his philosophy and those of Marx or Freud in mind: once we make the *double relation* (or the individualising and collectivising 'double relationship') the centre of the construction of a transindividuality that overcomes the dilemmas of classical ontology, it becomes paradoxically more difficult, at first sight, to reattach it to such a perspective. This is due to the fact that the 'composite' of passionate and rational relations that, according to Spinoza, determines different degrees of autonomy for individuals along with regimes of stability for political societies, is animated internally by a tendency to increase its power to act, which pushes it from inadequacy towards the adequacy of its own internal relations. If therefore a maximum adequacy is in view, it must correspond to a limit at which the intrinsic ambivalence of the passions would tend to disappear. It is true that one can still interpret such a regime both on the plane of ideas and on that of affects (in accordance with what the Spinozist tradition calls the victory of 'joyous passions' over 'sad passions'). But at this point, a second, much more problematic element intervenes: what Spinoza describes as the emergence of the *third kind of knowledge* (which is also a kind of life), distinct *both* from the imagination and from reason, represents a *jump* outside the social and political problematic that had found its fulfilment in the propositions of Part IV of the *Ethics* on *convenientia* and the mutual utility of men. This is reflected in particular by the renunciation of the vocabulary of *virtue* and *friendship* (based on *utility*) in favour of that of *beatitude* and *wisdom*.

Naturally, the problems of interpretation linked to this new 'transition', which is carried out by means of the understanding and according to the order it introduces into our thoughts and our affects (*ordinare ad intellectum*) are well known. I long believed (and have written)[44] that we could solve them by defining the 'third kind of knowledge' itself, not only as a form of life, but as a 'mode of communication'. This possibility no longer seems to me to be tenable once we think through the implications of Proposition 39, Part V, which makes the soul's ('partial') eternity correspond to an increase in the capacity to be affected by the *body proper*.[45] This does not mean that the Spinozist 'wise man' ought (in accordance with a Stoic tradition rejected by Spinoza) to be conceived of as *isolated*, or someone who isolates himself from society,[46] but that the increase of power evoked in the doctrine of Part V intensifies *individuality* as such, and not – at least not directly – the *relation* that involves the instance of the 'similar'. This is why I will say simultaneously that the existence of the third kind constitutes a *vanishing point* in relation to the previous relational structure analysed by Spinoza, and that it reveals (or invents) the possibility of an individuality which would be *in excess* in relation to transindividuality itself.

At this point, it is worth returning to our other authors to examine whether we can locate a problematic of the same kind there. Now, as far as Freud is concerned, the question has already in a sense been resolved, except that there the 'lines of flight' are in fact two in number, and the *excess* we are dealing with has an essentially *negative*, or even destructive, character, in accordance with the deep *pessimism* of Freudian anthropology (itself based on the positing of the 'death drive').[47] These lines of flight are situated in fact, *on the one hand*, on the side of 'mass formations' in an institutional direction, when it appears that they do *not always*, or do not completely, *repress* the phenomena of disconnection and violence against which they are constituted (panic, or more generally *social insecurity* in its various forms,[48] and intolerance or fanaticism of a religious or more generally ideological type); and on the other hand, as I have stressed in noting that there was on this point an enigmatic wavering of the Freudian terminology in the *Massenpsychologie*, on the at least hypothetical path which leads from neurosis to psychosis, that is to say, which abolishes individuals' capacity to resist the 'ferocity of the superego' that makes one feel guilty for satisfying the drives connected with life, and makes them fall into a state of incommunicability or defensive 'narcissism'.[49] By comparison, of course, the neurotic personality appears to also include a *positivity* (even when it is fraught with inhibitions, which belie the utopia of an 'untrammelled enjoyment'), which provides further justification for the Freudian idea that the isolation of the neurotic is a limit figure of the 'mass'. This fact prompts me to introduce another metaphor, alongside that of the 'line of flight', which is that of the *extreme edge* of transindividuality, where the 'relation' tends to turn into its opposite.

The most difficult case to treat from this perspective, of course, is that of Marx, whose conception of the transindividual might seem to be the most 'ontologically' unequivocal or, if you like, the least aleatory. And this is why, in recent commentary in particular, taking inspiration from Lukács and combining it as needed with concepts from Anglo-American analytical philosophy, a new generation have sought to read in Marx a *social ontology*.[50] This situation is insoluble as long as one cleaves to the conception elaborated by Marx in his youthful period, and reformulated in terms of the ontology of relations in the *Theses on Feuerbach* I commented on above. The situation is, then, one of 'all or nothing', in which the *social* (or 'relational') *essence* of the human individual (*das Ensemble der gesellschaftlichen Verhältnisse*) can be presented only in an 'alienated' (which is to say desocialised) form or in an 'emancipated' form, which for Marx is communist society, where individuals acts for one another as the upholders of the community that they all constitute together. But the problematic of 'commodity fetishism' (and above all of what I have called the *double fetishism* of 'things' and 'people', with the constitutive chiasm that it entails between the forms of economic alienation and those of juridical alienation) introduces new possibilities. Of course, this rests more than ever, in Marx's militant exposition, on the antithesis between the alienation of the present, inherent in commercial societies, and the image of the communist society to come, in which the division of social labour and the corresponding 'forms of individuality' would become objects of planning and more generally of a *conscious* organisation. Thus, taking as read the idea that what operates in Marx's analysis is a (critical) anthropology of *alienation as a relation constitutive of the 'social'*, outside of which, historically, individuals do not exist (even though they must always feel like they are 'strangers to themselves'), one could say that the *line of flight* is represented by the depiction of *utopian communism*, constantly intertwined with that of fetishism in Marx's analysis. But as this possibility of reversing alienation is presented at the same time by Marx as *immanent* in the movement of transformation, which is to say in the historical process in which contradictions develop and potentialities of the social relation are realised little by little,[51] one can say that communism constitutes an *internal surplus* of capitalism, or that the concept of it represents the extreme *edge* of transindividuality, for which Marx, through his analysis of commodity fetishism, defined the historical structure. And this conception even opens up the possibility of conceiving transgression or abolition (*Aufhebung*), not so much as a chronological substitution (as in the way in which classical 'evolutionist' Marxism imagined that, beyond the coming communist revolution, an entirely new type of social relations would one day emerge) but more as a mutation of the effect of society itself, which corresponds to an 'active' and 'performative' signification of the idea of utopia.[52] This way of understanding Marx (or of rectifying him) takes on its full meaning if one makes communism not so much a unilateral 'revenge' of the idea of community on bourgeois (and market) individualism, as a true *unity of opposites*, in which socialisation and individualisation, instead of being mutually exclusive, would become the components of a single social relation (or would ceaselessly reinforce each other). Such an idea can be identified with what I will call a *utopian transindividuality*, wherein the logical formula of the double critique (an ontology of the relation, neither individualist or atomist, nor collectivist or organicist) gives way to a hypothetical *double affirmation* (a 'relation' that posits *both* the autonomy of individuals *and* their mutual dependence). The political meaning of this utopia would not be to imagine another world, or to seek the restoration of a lost origin, but to stand permanently for the tendency, and better yet the *practical task* that 'orients' 'praxis' (which Marxism also refers to as 'struggle') internally for human subjects in capitalism – a perhaps impossible task, but constantly on the agenda, or impossible to dispel. Communism is the paradoxical unity of antinomic modes of existence that men (or *some* men) seek to achieve in their life, and for which they invest simultaneously in their struggles.

But, in its turn, this elucidation of the meaning that we can confer upon the hypothesis of a *limit* or of an *edge* of the transindividual, issuing from the comparison between Freud's 'pessimism' and Marx's 'utopianism', affords us one last occasion to look to Spinoza. I have argued that, in Parts IV and V of the *Ethics*, the analytic of the 'ratio' between the passionate and rational forces of the human essence makes way for the intuition of 'freedom' as a 'power of the understanding', immediately applied to an evidently privileged 'object' for the singular individual (since it is both the seat of its 'power' and its 'powerlessness'), namely the *body proper* in which their affections are located and whose mind forms more or less adequate ideas. This is fair, but it is incomplete, as careful re-reading of the Demonstration and Scholium of Part V, Proposition 39 shows: Spinoza in fact sets aside the previous transindividual 'ratio', in which the instance of reason within the passions and that, symmetrical if not equivalent, of the passions within reason, came from the relationship that each individual always maintains with those 'similar' to them. But at the same time, he establishes another, this time with *nature in general* (or if one wants, with God conceived as *natura naturata*, of which he is himself the effect). What makes something knowledge of the third kind is the fact that, *by understanding it*, the individual succeeds in conceiving their own bodily singularity as a 'part', one of a kind, and yet *equal to everything else*, of the system of multiple affections and of the communication of movements which define the whole of nature as an infinite (that is, open) totality. And thus it is entirely possible to suggest that Spinoza has suspended, or delimited, the analysis of the transindividual as a mode of sociability only to open up *another modality*, that which makes each individual a part of nature in a relation of mutual constitution with all the other parts, themselves individualised or individualisable. Up to this point I have stuck to the letter of Spinoza, but it is evidently very tempting, building on this, to take *a step beyond* what he says, if not beyond what he allows to be thought – at least as a *problem* – and which perhaps constitutes the edge of the edge, the 'utopian' moment of Spinozism itself: I will thus ask myself whether a possibility exists (and *for what*, for what 'kind of knowledge', or, rather, for what 'effort at knowledge') of conceiving *sub specie aeternitatis* the complex, conflicting *quasi-individuals* that are 'cities' with their singular 'regimes', or their more or less stable social and ideological combinations, and thus their 'history', as forming themselves *their own parts of nature*, or 'singular effects' of divine power. And one will ask oneself what such knowledge, generated from *inside* the city by its own 'citizens', *would change* in the life of these cities.[53]

To conclude, it seems to me that these comparative considerations, even if they involve an element of speculation, shed some light on what appeared from the beginning to be an essential characteristic of the philosophies of the transindividual that I call 'classical': the fact that they combine the depiction of the 'chiasm' or 'ratio' between different objective and subjective modalities of the 'social relation', with the hypothesis of an essential *mutability* (*Veränderbarkeit* in Marx, the transferential 'displacement' of neurotic identifications in Freud, and the increase or decrease of the power to act in Spinoza). The difficulty is always the same: this mutability must be *real* (or produce real effects) while remaining *immanent* in a certain 'structure' of relations, outside of which individuals do not simply *exist* as such, and of which the observable regime is always that of *alienation*. We must therefore renounce the possibility of returning to an originary freedom or spontaneity which would have been preserved in a redoubt or in an individual 'crypt', as well as dialectical illusions of a revolutionary destiny, the essential manifestation of which would be constituted by the evolution of the social 'whole'. What our three philosophers, or my readings of them, seem to show is that the *position* of this problem (and therefore the reflection of its intrinsically political nature, albeit that the term 'political' takes on a different sense with each thinker) is conditional on the possibility of identifying, within the 'relation', a *line of flight* with respect to its equilibrium or its constitutive symmetry. The other metaphor that I use points in the same direction: we must proceed *to the edge of the transindividual*, where it 'decomposes', or tends to exceed itself, by destabilising the figures of individuality and of community it instituted, to identify the possibility for its transformation without importing an ideal alternative from outside. This is also what allows me to say that the constructions of the transindividual in philosophy (and in politics) have a transcendental, or more precisely *quasi-transcendental* function.[54] They would constitute anthropological 'transcendentals' if their meaning was only to *render thinkable* the originary articulation of the individual and of the collective (or of the community) and the indefinitely varied empirical modalities of their establishment – which sometimes make the collective and more or less 'organic' solidarity primary, and sometimes give primacy to the individual or tend to isolate him, at least fictively – and if they were concerned to fix the *limits* of these variations (which we know well, however, are not determined *a priori*). But they correspond, rather, to a quasi-transcendental way of *problematising both the relation and the variation* as two aspects of the same problem, because they put in question (or make us question) both what *institutes* the individual or the collective in 'relation' with one another, and what never ceases to *denature* them, or to make them unrecognisable through the transgression of limits or the invention of modalities (which is to say the way human beings are 'individualised' while generating a 'society effect') which may be original, and for which it remains each time to evaluate their productiveness, or even their liveability.

## Notes

1 I will single out for mention the two collections that have appeared in Italy and Greece respectively: Étienne Balibar and Vittorio Morfino (eds), *Il transindividuale. Soggetti, Relazioni, Mutazioni* (Milan: Mimesis, 2014); and Michalis Bartsides (ed.), Διατομικότητα: Κείμενα για μία οντολογία της σχέσης, trans. Loukia Mano-Christidis (Athens: Nissos, 2014). I must of course reserve a special place for Jason Read's book, *The Politics of Transindividuality* (Leiden: Brill, 2016), not only because he does me the honour of devoting an entire treatment to my 'theses', in addition to many references to my readings of the classic works ('Transindividuality as politics in the thought of Étienne Balibar'), but because he puts together a magisterial appropriation of the problematic of the transindividual, marshalling a whole set of classical and contemporary references (except for Freud, who is the relevant index of a divergence between us) to construct a great 'transformation of philosophy' with a view to the 'transformation of the world'. I have learnt an immense amount from reading his book, which has stimulated greatly my desire to extend my previous analyses, and the echoes of which are ever-present in what follows.
2 The two parallel attempts, to which I allude here, are, respectively:, Étienne Balibar, *Spinoza: From Individuality to Transindividuality* (Delft: Eburon, 1997); and Étienne Balibar, 'From philosophical anthropology to social ontology and back: what to do with Marx's sixth thesis on Feuerbach?', *Postmodern Culture*, 22: 3 (2012), reproduced in Étienne Balibar, *The Philosophy of Marx* (London: Verso, 2017). In both cases, I am careful to note that the terminology of the transindividual has sources other than Simondon, even if they are less prominent, in particular Kojève and Lacan (so a certain reading of Hegel and a certain reading of Freud respectively). The contributors to the collective volume Balibar and Morfino (eds), *Il transindividuale*, have identified other sources, this time closer to Marxism: Vygotsky and Goldmann.
3 See Muriel Combes, *Simondon: individu et collectivité* (Paris: Presses universitaires de France, 1999), pp. 24, 92.
4 Sigmund Freud, *Massenpsychologie und Ich-Analyse* (Vienna: Internationaler Psychoanalytischer Verlag, 1921).
5 *Ethics* Part III.
6 See Balibar, *The Philosophy of Marx*.
7 The *1844 Manuscripts*.
8 I have thought I could consider as symptomatic, from this point of view,

the fact that in Thesis 6 Marx uses the floating term (transposed from French) *das Ensemble*, instead of speaking in terms of the totality or system. By comparison, when Marx returns to the foundational notion of 'social relations' in the Preface to the *Contribution to the Critique of Political Economy* of 1859, it will be given a very strong (and very restrictive) determination: 'in the social production of their life, people enter . . . into relations of production' ('In der gesellschaftlichen Produktion ihres Lebens gehen die Menschen bestimmte, notwendige, von ihrem Willen unabhängige Verhältnisse ein, Produktionsverhältnisse').

9 This is obviously inspired by the Hegelian dialectical *zugleich*. See Karl Marx (1867), *Capital*, trans. Ben Fowkes (London: Penguin, 1976), vol. 1, pp. 929–30.

10 I borrow the expression 'society effect' from Louis Althusser, who used it at the end of his Preface to the collective volume *Reading Capital*, to mark the philosophical difference between Marx's analysis and theories which view society as a collective subject or as an aggregate of individual actions, hence in an implicitly 'transindividualist' way, but without developing this implication. Althusser, moreover, is notoriously hostile to taking up the theme of the 'fetishism of the commodity' in his critical reading of Marx. Louis Althusser and Étienne Balibar (eds), *Lire le capital* (Paris: Maspero, 1965).

11 The idea that Hegel would 'displace' the dialectic of subject and object in order to internalise it in the history of the subject to the detriment of the question of the object and objects (or of the conflict between materiality and sensible appearance that they imply) – a displacement that needs to be reversed with Marx or to better understand Marx – appears in the Adorno's *Negative Dialectics*.

12 The fourth 'Thesis' on Feuerbach already contains a concept of 'doubling' or 'redoubling of the world' (by religious or political representations) to which Georges Labica, in particular, devotes a profound commentary. Georges Labica, *Les Thèses sur Feuerbach* (Paris: Presses universitaires de France, 1987).

13 Marx, *Capital*, pp. 165–6, Section I, Chapter 1 ('The commodity'), Section 4 ('The fetishism of the commodity and its secret').

14 Chapter 1 of book I, on 'The process of exchange', which nevertheless immediately follows the exposition of the fetishism of the commodity. In the reading I propose – as I have already in Balibar, *The Philosophy of Marx* – the section on the 'fetishism of the commodity' at the end of Chapter 1 and Chapter 2 constitute the two parts of the same philosophical

'mediation' between the development of the commodity form and the general equivalent, in Chapter 1, and the analysis of the properties of the money form (or currency) in Chapter 3.

15  These categories are those of 'Roman law', extended to the bourgeois era. The description that Marx gives of this extension follows closely Hegel's exposition in the initial section of the 1821 *Philosophy of Right* on 'abstract right'. What belongs to it in its own right is the articulation with the structures of production and exchange.

16  Marx, *Capital*, p. 179. Such theatrical terminology constitutes a rich vein running through the Western philosophical and juridical tradition, coming from Stoic philosophy and founded on the double usage of the Latin word *persona* (person – *prosopon* in Greek) incorporated in Roman law which distinguishes 'persons' into free and dependent ones.

17  Read, *The Politics of Transindividuality*, pp. 74ff.

18  There is an obvious affinity between the Spinozist construction and the Platonic constitution (in the *Republic*) of the 'correspondence' between the composition of individual souls (writ 'small') and that of the city itself (writ 'large') with regard to justice and injustice. This nevertheless does not imply a singular interpretation of the Spinozist schema: I return to this below.

19  This decomposition is death. But we know, by the famous Scholium of the 'Spanish poet' after Proposition 39 of Part IV, that, for Spinoza, death is a change of form that can be understood in multiple senses. François Zourabichbili, in particular, interprets this masterfully in his *Le conservatism paradoxal de Spinoza: Enfance et royauté* (Paris: Presses universitaires de France, 2002).

20  The power to act as the capacity to be affected proportional to this capacity: this is the last word of Spinoza's metaphysics, and in itself the most revolutionary proposition of his philosophy, understood as an ethics.

21  I am referring here to the thesis of Chapter 3 above. Once again, all these developments constitute to a large extent a dialogue with Alexandre Matheron, taking into account in particular the evolution of his views on the question of *individuality* in the 'physical' sense of the body politic in Spinoza.

22  Part IV, Proposition 18, Scholium.

23  Translator's note: in Curley's English translation this phrase is typically rendered as 'everyone' – which paradoxically of course does not uncomplicatedly connote a single individual. Balibar points to the French translation as *chacun*, literally 'each one', which is the phrase Elwes's English translation uses to render Spinoza's phrase.

24 The ideal democracy, of which Spinoza did not furnish a description in the 'missing' chapter of the *Political Treatise*, is presented in this sense as a 'totally absolute' (omnino absolutum) form of state (*imperium*).
25 In Part II (especially Chapter 3) of his book *Spinoza: L'expérience et l'éternité* (Paris: Presses universitaires de France, 1994), Pierre-François Moreau gives an analysis, unsurpassable in my eyes, of the constitution of this 'unanimity' and of its institutional modalities, its fluctuations and its limits in Spinoza.
26 This key term by which, in accordance with its Latin etymology, one should understand not only a 'mutual agreement' but the fact of *coming to the same point*, or of coming together. It is also the word that Cicero proposed to 'translate' the central concept of Stoicism, *oikeiôsis*.
27 See in particular the Chantal Jaquet's contributions in *Spinoza à l'œuvre. Composition des corps et force des idées* (Paris: Publications de la Sorbonne, 2017) and Frédéric Lordon's (in my opinion less rigorous) ones in *La société des affects. Pour un structuralisme des passions* (Paris: Editions du Seuil, 2013).
28 The notion of 'transition' was proposed in particular by Vittorio Morfino during our discussions to prepare the collective volume mentioned above. I find it excellent. One cannot, of course, but think of making a comparison with Marx's *Veränderbarkeit*.
29 Here, too, one reads a proposition of an ontological nature within the political anthropology: it is the application of the Axiom of Part IV, the position of which therefore seems extraordinarily deliberate since Part IV makes it a theory of sociability.
30 The key formulation is in the appendix of Part IV of the *Ethics*, Chapter 26: 'Apart from men we know [or encounter: 'novimus'] no singular thing ['nihil singular'] in Nature whose mind we can enjoy, and which we can join to ourselves in friendship, or some kind of association ['aliquo consuetudinis genere']. And so whatever there is in Nature apart from men, the principle of seeking our own advantage does not demand that we preserve it.' In *Spinoza and the Politics of Renaturalization* (Chicago: University of Chicago Press, 2011), Hasana Sharp discusses in a very interesting way the problems posed, symmetrically, by the extension of the notion of utility to the whole of nature and its restriction to 'human nature', which brings Spinoza close to a 'politics of the gratitude'. See also the 'ambiguity' that Pierre Macherey, in his commentary on Proposition 36 of Part IV of the *Ethics*, believes can characterise the way in which Spinoza's *universalism* is related to the criterion of the 'same nature' that all men must 'possess'. Pierre Macherey, *Introduction à l'Ethique de Spinoza. La quatrième partie: la condition humaine* (Paris: Presses universitaires de France, 1997), p. 214.

31 It is striking that Spinoza also inscribes at this junction the efficacy of other notions of historical or institutional character, first of all *religion*, which is split in *piety* (*pietas*) and *morality* (*honestas*) reproducing in the gap between these the idea of a double relation, or of a ratio, and reminding us once more that everything 'read' in the institutions of the city must also be 'read' in the analysis of the fluctuations of the character of the individuals .

32 See my 'The invention of the superego: Freud and Kelsen, 1922', in *Citizen Subject: Foundations for Philosophical Anthropology* (New York: Fordham University Press, 2017).

33 And not just in a *political unconscious*, as Pierre Kaufmann writes in what remains, however, a beautiful book. Pierre Kaufmann, *L'inconscient du politique* (Paris: Presses universitaires de France, 1979).

34 Sigmund Freud, *Mass Psychology and Other Writings* [1921], trans. J. A. Underwood (London: Penguin, 2004), Chapter 8: 'Verliebtheit und Hypnose'.

35 'In you more than you', as Jacques Lacan says in Seminar XI: *The Four Fundamental Concepts of Psychoanalysis* (New York: Norton, 1981).

36 Not without strongly evoking the Simmel's descriptions in the preceding period, in that it makes the elucidation of 'couples' and their modality of 'liaison' (or their own *eros*) the pivot of the whole construction.

37 In a note in Chapter 4, in the 1923 edition, Freud defends himself against Kelsen's charge of having hypostatised 'society' in the fashion of Durkheim.

38 On these antitheses, one should obviously consult Georges Canguilhem's work; not only his historical work, *The Normal and Pathological* (Dordrecht: D. Reidel, 1978), but the later essays collected in the volume *Writings on Medicine* (New York: Fordham University Press, 2012).

39 The concept of the 'primary' process as elaborated in Freud's 1900 *Traumdeutung* (*On the Interpretation of Dreams*) refers to the association of ideas and mechanisms of emotional investment that obey without inhibition or 'secondary elaboration' to the laws of the unconscious.

40 I will use the term 'impolitics', after Thomas Mann and Roberto Esposito, to designate the reverse of irrationality, which is indissociable from political rationality itself. See my *Violence and Civility* (New York: Columbia University Press, 2015).

41 This is evoked by Paul Federn in a pamphlet which immediately antedates Freud's book, *Zur Psychologie der Revolution: Die Vaterlose Gesellschaft* (1919), to which I think Freud, at least partly, is reacting, although without stating this.

42 In Althusser's terminology – Louis Althusser, 'Idéologie et appareils

idéologiques d'État', in *Sur la reproduction* (Paris: Presses universitaires de France, 2011), pp. 138–72 (which is obviously much inspired by this text of Freud's) – the army and the Church could be said to constitute two great 'ideological state apparatuses' whose internal spring is the structure of libidinal love for the real or imaginary 'leader' (*Führer*), or that they together form what would have to be called *the ideological state apparatus*, at its essentially unconscious source. But then the question cannot not be asked as to why Freud *evades* reference to the state as such, while his whole analysis supposes it, thus contributing to the possibility of 'depoliticising' his analysis of politics – at least in the eyes of those for whom the concept of politics is inseparable from a reference to the state. See again Balibar, 'The invention of the superego'.

43 However, this negative modality seems to haunt the idea that the reverse side of institutions (or the object of their resistance) is their own pathological decomposition.

44 In particular on the chapter on 'modes of communication' appended to my book *Spinoza and Politics* for the English edition. Étienne Balibar, *Spinoza and Politics*, trans. Peter Snowdon (New York: Verso, 1998).

45 Spinoza, *Ethics*, Part V, Proposition 39: 'Qui corpus ad plurima aptum habet, is mentem habet, cujus maxima pars est aeterna' (He who has a Body capable of a great many things has a Mind whose greatest part is eternal).

46 Yet there are propositions of Spinoza's that point in this direction, especially Part IV, Proposition 70: 'Homo liber, qui inter ignaros vivit, eorum, quantum potest, beneficia declinare studet' (A free man who lives among the ignorant strives, as far as he can, to avoid their favours).

47 This assumes that the Freudian 'death drive' (*Todestrieb*) be read exclusively in terms of the destruction or aggression (to others and to oneself). If we also consider its radically 'pacifying' side (its tendency to negate instinctual arousal), it must also contain a radical ambivalence.

48 I am intentionally alluding to the title of a book in which Robert Castel, examining the crisis of the contemporary 'social state', is interested in forms *of negative individuality* and the *disaffiliation* it generates. R. Castel, *L'insécurité sociale* (Paris: Seuil, 2003).

49 These hypotheses result from a cursory comparison of Freud's texts concerning the 'superego', the 'split of the ego' and melancholia. A profound analysis of the ambivalence of narcissism can be found in André Green, *Narcissisme de vie, narcissisme de mort* (Paris: Editions de Minuit, 1983).

50 I am thinking here in particular of Frédéric Monferrand's thesis 'Ontologie

sociale et théorie critique chez Marx', 2015, the imminent publication of which is to be hoped for.
51 In accordance with the great formula of his youth (from *The German Ideology*) never disavowed by Marx: 'We call communism the real movement which abolishes the present state of things'.
52 This is essentially Mannheim's view, which several contemporary commentators have dealt with: see in particular Pierre Macherey, *De l'utopie!* (Le Havre: De l'incidence, 2011).
53 It would require a little extra time and space to explain what such an 'ultra-Spinozist' hypothesis can have in common with a discussion of the consequences of the fact that, in Proposition 37 of Part V, Spinoza 'lifts' the condition which he had stated in the single Axiom of Part IV: 'Nulla res singularis in rerum natura datur, qua potentior and fortior non detur alia. Sed quacunque data datur alia potentior, a qua illa data potest destrui.' If this 'naturalistic' thesis is placed at the front of the part of the *Ethics* in which Spinoza develops his theory of sociability, this is obviously to explain that the existence of cities constitutes the means for human individuals to *protect* themselves from the destructive capacities of the surrounding nature, or to advance *the alliance with nature* to the detriment of the *competition between man and other natural individuals* (I certainly wish today, from the point of view of an ecological critique of environmental destruction, that this were the case). But it is also to explain that this extension and this protection *have limits* and remain affected by finitude. However, it remains for us to ask how these limits can be *displaced*, and above all what price in terms of 'conscious' modifications to the internal economy of the cities would be required. This is a question of some contemporary relevance. It could also be that Spinoza 'fails' to formalise (or 'constitutionalise') the democratic regime in the *Political Treatise* because he himself misunderstood the meaning of the notion of an *imperium omnino absolutum* (*Political Treatise* 11.1) and yet always 'finishes' with regard to nature. This is not *another type of 'constitution'*, but a *question* about the sense in which political institutions evolve when they move beyond the 'division of powers' as a method of rationalising affective fluctuations.
54 In contemporary philosophy, the notion of the 'quasi-transcendental' has been employed notably by Foucault and Derrida, although in two senses that seem different at first sight. For Foucault, the quasi-transcendental is a system of conditions of possibility (an 'historical *a priori*') that is constantly modified (one could say 'contaminated') by its own empirical realisations. For Derrida, the quasi-transcendental is a system of 'conditions of

possibility' which are at the same time 'conditions of impossibility', that is to say, imply both the construction and the destruction, or *the uncertainty* of the forms of life and thought between these two opposites. I try to make use of it by taking it to imply something like the idea of a *relationship of transgression* to the constitutive relationship itself.

# Select Bibliography

Adorno, T. (1973) [1966], *Negative Dialectics*, London: Routledge.
Althusser, Louis (2011), 'Idéologie et appareils idéologiques d'État', in *Sur la reproduction*, Paris: Presses universitaires de France, pp. 138–72.
Althusser, Louis, and Étienne Balibar (eds) (1965), *Lire le capital*, Paris: Maspero.
Balibar, Étienne (1997), *Spinoza: From Individuality to Transindividuality*, Delft: Eburon.
Balibar, Étienne (1998) [1985], *Spinoza and Politics*, London: Verso.
Balibar, Étienne (2001), 'Potentia multitudinis, quae una veluti mente ducitur', in Marcel Senn and Manfred Walther (eds), *Ethik, Recht and Politik bei Spinoza*, Zürich: Schulthess, pp. 105–37.
Balibar, Étienne (2012), 'From philosophical anthropology to social ontology and back: what to do with Marx's sixth thesis on Feuerbach?', *Postmodern Culture*, 22:3, reproduced in Balibar (2017).
Balibar, Étienne (2017), *The Philosophy of Marx*, London: Verso.
Balibar, Étienne, and Vittorio Morfino (eds) (2014), *Il transindividuale. Soggetti, Relazioni, Mutazioni*, Milan: Mimesis.
Bartsides, Michalis (ed.) (2014), *Διατομικότητα: Κείμενα για μία οντολογία της σχέσης*. trans. Loukia Mano-Christidis, Athens: Nissos.
Combes, M. (1999), *Simondon: individu et collectivité*, Paris: Presses universitaires de France.
Freud, Sigmund (1921), *Massenpsychologie und Ich-Analyse*, Vienna: Internationaler Psychoanalytischer Verlag.
Freud, Sigmund (1922) [1921], *Group Psychology and the Analysis of the Ego*, trans. James Strachey, London: Hogarth.
Freud, Sigmund (2004) [1921], *Mass Psychology and Other Writings*, trans. J. A. Underwood, London: Penguin.

## SELECT BIBLIOGRAPHY

Gueroult, Martial (1968), *Spinoza, Volume I*, Hildesheim: Georg Olms Verlag.
Gueroult, Martial (1974), *Spinoza, Volume II*, Hildesheim: Georg Olms Verlag.
Le Bon, Gustave (1895), *La psychologie des foules*, Paris: Alcan.
Marx, Karl (1976) [1867], *Capital*, Volume 1, trans. Ben Fowkes, London: Penguin.
Moreau, Pierre-François (1994), *Spinoza: l'expérience et l'éternité*, Paris: Presses universitaires de France.
Negri, Antonio (1981), *L'anomolia Selvaggia: Saggio su potere e potenza in Baruch Spinoza*, Milan: Feltrinelli.
Read, Jason (2016), *The Politics of Transindividuality*, Leiden: Brill.
Spinoza (1996) [1677], *Ethics*, trans. Edwin M. Curley, London: Penguin.

# Index

Althusser, Louis, xii, xvi–xvii, 33, 129, 143, 153, 185, 188
Appuhn, Charles, 96, 123
Aquinas, Thomas, 33
Aristotle, 5–6, 10, 36, 43, 80–1, 84, 90, 135–6

Bloch, Ernst, 143, 145
Bove, Laurent, 103
Boyle, Robert, 7

Canguilhem, Georges, 188
Castel, Robert, 189
Christ, Jesus, 173
Combes, Muriel, 138
*conatus*, 4, 15, 20, 29, 36–7, 39, 44, 49, 52, 54, 57, 65, 69, 72, 83–4, 203, 105, 109, 114–15, 127, 157–9, 162
consciousness, 38–40, 52, 60, 61, 76, 78–9, 117

Cristolfini, Paolo, 94–5, 123, 132, 136, 138, 158

Deleuze, Gilles, 71–2, 89, 124, 134,
Democritus, 5
Derrida, Jacques, 190
Descartes, René, 5–6, 8–9, 11, 14, 18, 22, 35, 51, 83

Epicurus, 5
Esposito, Roberto, 188

Federn, Paul, 188
Foucault, Michel, 190
Freud, Sigmund, 190

Galileo, 11
Giancotti, Boscherini Emilia, 129
God, 9, 14, 19–24, 32–4, 36, 40, 43, 46–8, 67, 70, 75, 78, 85, 89, 131, 155, 181

# INDEX

Gueroult, Martial, 15, 33–4, 80, 82–4

Hegel, G. W. F., xv–xvi, 41, 105, 141, 184–6
Hobbes, Thomas, 41, 71, 79, 103, 112, 120, 124, 127, 131, 159
Husserl, Edmund, 72, 79, 91

individualisation, 43, 61, 78, 80, 119, 168, 170
individuation, xvi–xvii, 4, 27, 30, 43–5, 56, 61, 72, 78, 80–1, 86–7, 98, 101, 105, 119, 131, 138–9, 157, 170
*ingenium*, 68, 113–14, 118–19, 129–30

Kant, Immanuel, 22, 27, 46–7, 49, 79, 81, 83, 91
Kaufmann, Pierre, 188

Lacan, Jacques, 184, 188
Lazzeri, Christian, 103
Le Bon, Gustave, 170–1
Leibniz, Gottfried Wilhelm, 11–12, 14, 71–3, 75, 79–80, 83, 91
Locke, John, 41, 79, 152
Lucretius, 5
Lukács, György, xiii, 178

Macherey, Pierre, 31, 82–3, 97, 135–6, 187, 190
Machiavelli, Niccolò, 114, 118, 135, 161, 164
McShea, Robert J., 105
Mann, Thomas, 188
Marx, Karl, xii–xiii, xv, xx–xxi, 105, 138, 141–55, 166, 175–6, 178–80, 182, 184–7
Matheron, Alexandre, xiii–xvii, 40–2, 75, 80, 86, 90, 93, 101–4, 109, 114–15, 125, 133–5, 137, 163, 186
Menenius, Agrippa, 100
*mens*, 61, 84, 87, 92–100, 112, 115, 117, 121–4, 128–32
metaphor, 85, 98, 103, 107, 114, 178, 183
metaphysics, 5, 15–16, 30, 40, 75, 81, 84, 108, 112, 127, 139, 186
Moreau, Pierre-François, 93–5, 101, 112–20, 129, 131–5, 187

nature, xiv–xv, xvii, xix, 5, 8–12, 22, 29, 32, 36, 43, 46, 48, 50–2, 60, 69, 71, 74, 79, 83, 96, 106–7, 137, 139, 155, 157, 181–2, 187, 190

Negri, Antonio, 15–16, 79, 81, 86, 93, 107–12, 126–7, 133–4, 165
Newton, Isaac, 11, 34

Oldenburg, Henry, 9–11, 14
ontology, 3–6, 15–16
organicism, 40–1, 44–5, 50, 104

physics, 6–7, 10–11, 14–16, 33-4, 52, 81–2, 84, 106, 121, 134
politics, 53, 69, 79, 85, 101–2, 104–7, 111, 127, 131–3, 137, 140–1, 154–5, 166, 172, 183

Read, Jason, xii–xxi, 141, 154, 158, 175, 184
reason, 46, 58–9, 61, 64–9, 78, 110–11, 113, 117, 123, 134, 156–7, 163–5, 176, 181
Rice, Lee C., 93, 98, 104–7, 114, 130, 134–5

Rousseau, Jean-Jacques, 110, 127

science, 3, 11, 60, 106, 134, 170
Sharp, Hasana, 187
Simondon, Gilbert, xiii–xv, 45, 47, 57, 80–2, 86–7, 137–9, 184
substance, 3–7, 9, 13–32, 43, 47, 51, 77, 79, 95, 128, 131, 139, 144, 161, 164

Tacitus, 116, 161
Tschirnhaus, Ehrenfried Walther von, 12–14, 16, 19, 29, 32, 34

Uyl, Den Douglas, 105

whole, 4, 7–10, 14–15, 32–3, 50–1, 64, 72, 74, 77, 80, 96, 105, 114, 126, 174, 181–2
Wittgenstein, Ludwig, 31, 33

EU representative:
Easy Access System Europe
Mustamäe tee 50, 10621 Tallinn, Estonia
Gpsr.requests@easproject.com

www.ingramcontent.com/pod-product-compliance
Lightning Source LLC
Chambersburg PA
CBHW070354240426
43671CB00013BA/2495